THE TAILGATE COOKBOOK

75 GAME-CHANGING RECIPES FOR THE TASTIEST TAILGATE EVER

BETH PETERSON

THE TAILGATE COOKBOOK

75 GAME-CHANGING RECIPES FOR THE TASTIEST TAILGATE EVER

The Deviled Bacon

Front Table Books
An imprint of Cedar Fort, Inc.
Springville, Utah

ISBN 13: 978-1-4621-2223-3

Published by Front Table Books, an imprint of Cedar Fort, Inc.
2373 W. 700 S., Springville, UT, 84663
Distributed by Cedar Fort, Inc., www.cedarfort.com

Library of Congress Cataloging-in-Publication Data

Names: Peterson, Beth, 1967- author.
Title: The tailgate cookbook : 75 game-changing recipes for the tastiest
    tailgate ever / Beth Peterson.
Description: Springville, Utah : Front Table Books, An imprint of Cedar Fort,
    Inc., [2018] | Includes index.
Identifiers: LCCN 2018018010 (print) | LCCN 2018019990 (ebook) | ISBN
    9781462129058 (epub, pdf, mobi) | ISBN 9781462122233 | ISBN
    9781462122233 q(perfect bound : qalk. paper)
Subjects: LCSH: Tailgate parties. | Outdoor cooking. | LCGFT: Cookbooks.
Classification: LCC TX823 (ebook) | LCC TX823 .P4555 2018 (print) | DDC
    642/.3--dc23
LC record available at https://lccn.loc.gov/2018018010
Cover and page design by Shawnda T. Craig
Cover design © 2018 Cedar Fort, Inc.
Edited by Nicole Terry

Printed in the United States of America

10 9 8 7 6 5 4 3 2 1

Printed on acid-free paper

2, 4, 6, 8!
HERE'S WHO I APPRECIATE!

To my personal cheerleaders:

This book is dedicated to the three loves of my life: Alex, Luke, and Francesca—my two tough football players and my sweet princess. Everything I do, I do for you.

CONTENTS

Introduction 1 • Chapter 1: Tailgate Glory 7 • Chapter 2: Training Camp 15

CHAPTER 3: PREGAME
DEVILED EGGS, DIPS, WINGS

Grilled Chicken Wings with Dr. BBQ's Alabama
White Sauce 30

Buffalo Cauliflower Nuggets 31

Ginger Sticky Chicken Drummettes 32

The Bloody Mary Jell-O Shot—alcohol free 34

Shrimp and Peach Ceviche 36

Sushi Donuts 37

The Classic Deviled Egg 38

"Lobster Roll" Deviled Egg 40

Chipotle Cilantro Deviled Egg 41

Fire-Roasted Jalapeño Deviled Egg 42

The Deviled Bacon 44

The Down South Pimento Cheese & Jalapeño
Deviled Egg 47

BLT Dip 48

Grilled Corn, Bacon, and Chipotle Dip 49

Grilled Romaine Lettuce with Heirloom Tomato
and Roasted Garlic Vinaigrette 50

Rosemary & Roasted Garlic White Bean Dip 53

Spiced Crab 54

The 1950s' Green Onion Dip 55

The Big, Bad Sriracha Fried Chickpea Hummus 56

Yo, It's Pepperoni Pizza Dip 57

CHAPTER 4: SIDELINE ACTION
NACHOS, THE SUPER CHAR-"CUTE"-RIE,
MAC DADDY MAC & CHEESE

Dijon Sliders with Caramelized Onions 62

Pimento Cheese Jalapeños Wrapped in Bacon 64

Mac Daddy Mac & Cheese 65

Warning! Ridiculously Addictive Blue Cheese
   Kettle Chips 67

The Classic Ham and Swiss Sandwich 68

Chorizo & Bean Sheet-Pan Nachos 71

Chunky Chili Nachos 72

Easy Delicious Refried Black Beans 74

Chunky Nacho Chili 75

Kari's Vegan Loaded Nachos 77

Mexican Braised Short Ribs 78

Mexican Braised Short Rib Sheet-Pan Nachos 79

Vegan Queso 80

Horseradish Sour Cream 81

Serrano Sweet Pepper Jelly 82

Pickled Red Onions 83

Guacamole 84

Elote Guacamole with Cilantro Crema 85

Pomegranate Guacamole 87

Roasted Tomatillo Guacamole 88

Cheddar Cheese Dip in a Bread Bowl 91

Bacon & Cheddar Soft Pretzels with Bacon
   Mustard Dip 92

How to Build an Ultimate Tailgate Char-"Cute"-rie ... 94

CHAPTER 5: GAME TIME!
THE HEARTY BITES

Adobo Lamb Pops with a Char-Roasted Poblano Dipping Sauce 100

Ally's Southern Heat—Spicy Pork Chops 103

Bacon Pimento Jalapeño Cheese Sandwich on a Pretzel Bun 104

Buffalo Chicken Pizza with Caramelized Red Onions ... 106

Caprese Pesto Trifle 108

Corned Beef Swiss and Coleslaw Sliders 109

Egg and Potato Bundlers—Bacon 110

Egg and Potato Bundlers—Chorizo 112

Egg and Potato Bundlers—Maple Sausage 113

Jay's Blackberry Bone-in Boston Butt 114

Lamar Moore's KFC—Korean Fried Chicken 116

E3VIP Fire Shrimp 118

Momma's Potato Salad 119

Sweet Heat Pulled Pork and Udon Noodles 120

Kerry's Big Bite Pastrami with Pancetta Giardiniera and Artichoke Spread 122

CHAPTER 6: THE EXTRA POINT DIY TAILGATE PARTY

Beth's Chili with Mushrooms & Black Beans 128

Game-Day Chili 131

Italian Chili Mac 132

White Chicken Chili Mac Bread Bowls 135

Chili Bar 136

Poppin' Popcorn Recipes 138

Roasted Poblano and Cheddar Cornbread in a
    Cast-Iron Skillet 141

Beth's Grilled Apple Cider Donuts with a Maple
    Glaze 142

Fried Chicken and Waffles Cupcakes 144

The Hot Chocolate Grill Cupcake 147

Hot Wing Cupcakes with Blue Cheese Frosting 148

The Meatloaf Cupcake 150

The Cheeseburger Brownie Cupcake 152

Donut and Cupcake Bar 154

The DIY Baggie Omelette 156

Danish Ebleskiver Waffles 158

Waffle Bites 160

Touchdown Brunch 162

Touchdown Brunch DIY Waffle Brunch Bar 164

CHAPTER 7: END-ZONE DANCE GAME-DAY DESSERTS

Cherry Cream Cheese Hand Pies 170

Jerry James Stone's Coconut, Lime, and Avocado
    Popsicles 173

Emily Ellyn's Peanut Butter Caramel Cheesecake 174

S'mores Cookie Sandwich 175

Honeycrisp Apple Panna Cotta 176

Killer Chunk Chocolate Cake with Chocolate
    Buttercream Frosting 178

Mini Apple Pies in a Jar 181

Peach Bread with Cheddar Crumble 182

The 50/50 Bar 184

The Slurping Watermelon 187

CHAPTER 8: ALL AMERICAN TAILGATE RECIPES FROM AROUND THE COUNTRY

Southern Sweet Tea 193

Whitney's Gator Corndogs 194

VV's Philly Cheesesteak Sliders 197

Bacon Cheeseburger Tater Tot Shepherd's Pie 199

Slow Cooker Chicago Italian Beef Sandwiches 200

Norwegian Beef and Veggie Stew
    (Brun Lapskaus) 203

Brown Bag Salmon 205

Mike's Crab, Shrimp, and Andouille Gumbo Dip 207

Hot Muffuletta Dip 208

Open Flame Char Oysters 210

Cute Roasted Baby Potatoes Stuffed with Shrimp
    and Bacon 213

Texas Gold Carne con Queso Dip 215

Index 219 • Notes 222
About the Photographer 223 • About the Author 224

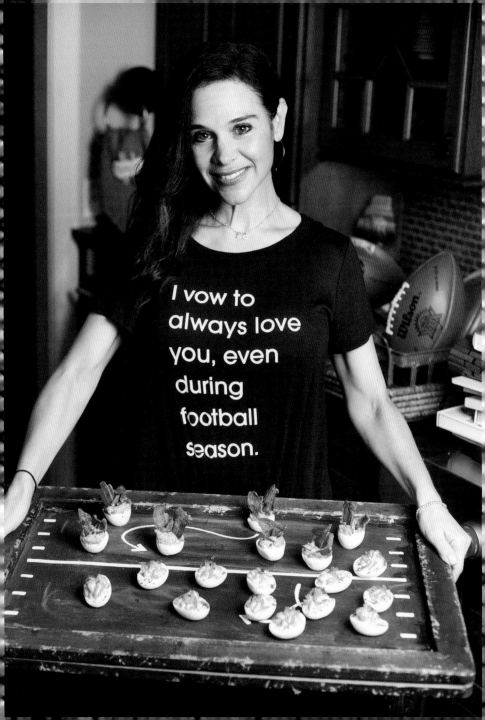

ACKNOWLEDGMENTS

Along the way, so many people have helped me get this book published. It's so much more than just a tailgate cookbook to me. The experience creating it has been a journey lined with gifts of love and support from my many friends and family. You've listened and encouraged as I moved my way through each step. You gave advice and lent your time, your goods, your kitchens, your bellies, your honest taste buds, and, in some cases, your substantial talents.

The very first person I must acknowledge is Mark Hartman, the photographer extraordinaire, for taking on the project. Your talent and your unending patience and kindness are why this project happened. The images are beautiful. I'm certain that the decision on the half tuck will be what makes this book a best seller.

Next, my love and thanks goes to Mom and Dad—the original party couple—your love for entertaining and bringing people together made me who I am.

Thank you to Kerry, the best sister a girl could have, and Thank you, to my dear Bostwicks—thanks Gabby for giving Aunt Betty the likes on Insta, and to AP, UJ, and the cousins. It's been fun to have had cheerleaders at every turn while writing the book. Thank you all, Muah!

Thanks to the brilliant marketer and my friend, Larry Oliphant, who introduced me to me to all of this tailgate fun.

Hugs and thanks to my personal valet, sous chef and bestie, you know, without you this book would not have gotten done. You've been so very good to me. Words really won't work here. True gratitude for such a wonderful friend, Thank you, Lara Bruce.

A special mention to my sweet friend at the gazebo – Who knew bingo tailgating could be so much fun? Big hugs.

To Dane Neal, for excellent greeting evaluations and unending encouragement.

To my great pal Dan "The Man" Stevenson, who wouldn't rest until I was employed.

To the ever-generous Amy and Lisa—my hometown ladies of the gorgeous Liam Brex (the official *The Tailgate Cookbook* test kitchen).

Thanks to Loretta at Looks for making me look tailgate pretty and to Bruce Singer and Cody Panfil for bringing your gorgeous vintage pickup trucks and for staying for the day.

To VV from DD my dance teacher for the last thirty-five years. I'm so lucky to have you as my life-time friend. Remember the country décor phase? This book is that but way better.

To each and every member of my Commission Sisters—you girls have been supporting my hairbrained schemes since the beginning and I love you for it.

To EC, for the daily check-ins and support.

To Amaury and Trish and their guest cave.

Thanks to Karly and Chris's Angels for putting up with the scary pics of me when I was in the thick of it.

Last, but not least, to Diane Jacob who believed I could, and was happily surprised when I did :)

Some big thank yous to my chef friend contributors from around the country:

To the hipster Santa Claus himself, the king of the Big Green Egg, the ruler of the Dr. BBQ restaurant, celebrity BBQ hall-of-famer, my friend and mentor, Dr. BBQ-Ray Lampe—your guidance and friendship has meant so much. Thank you for the wing recipe.

To my ride-or-die BFF, Kari Karch—way too much to say here; plus, you already know. Girl, you brought the house down with your tasty riff on vegan tailgate fun food. It's like you've done this before. Love ya always—Muah!

My dear, boldly boho, *Master Chef* roomie, Ally Phillips—always gently (and sometimes straight-up) telling me the ways of the world. We started down this foodie path together. It lead me to so many fun adventures with you and now, to this! Da recipe, it's real boho quality, babe—love it!

Master Chef superstar Whitney Miller—here's to the night in Vegas when we attempted to explain the Deep South to the man from Japan and to your recipe contribution that demonstrates the Deep South perfectly. Alligator anyone?

Chef Lamar Moore, for jumping in without question and just helping and for the KFC recipe contribution! Made it, ate it, loved it. Couldn't stop talking about it. Also, I'm not sure I know a nicer person than you. Thanks for adding to the fun!

Jerry James Stone for being California-cool and bringing the fresh vegetarian recipes that make us want to tailgate like a vegetarian. You rock!

Jay Ducote, the king of all things Louisiana food and LSU tailgate! Lucky us to have your delicious recipe captured in this book. Thank you! My stop at your EPIC tailgate at LSU inspired me to share how community is built by gathering folks around amazing regional foods!

Aimee Broussard—your southern hospitality welcomed us with open arms, and you're right, that Baton Rouge, Doberge Cake was one I'll never forget. Also, I'll never forget your sweet lil aunt in the "Go to Hell Ol' Miss" sweatshirt! *cutie! Thanks for the recipe, love.

My 100 percent retro rad and always sunshiny celebrity-chef pal, Emily Ellyn—Peanut Butter Cheesecake? Decadence with a twist! A true-blue winner! Love ya, girlie.

Thank you, Richard Carrier, for the delicious recipe. I'm so excited to have the legend of luxury tailgating represented. Also, thanks for helping us all to respect our package. Curious what that means? Check out Richard and his current project online.

A big shout-out to the Cedar Fort Publishing team for taking on this project!

Thank you all from the bottom of my lil tailgatin' heart.

INTRODUCTION

#GoTeamTailgate #Yay! #StyleUpYourTailgate
#NextLevelGrub

The number-one goal for a tailgate cook is to make a dish so beloved that it receives "legendary" status when put up against the plethora of typical bites on the tailgate table. The recipes in this book are here as inspiration, leading cooks to think bigger and bolder, moving past the expected, giving an edge on tailgate chef glory. Competition in the stadium drives the competitive culture in tailgate cooking. Like the players on the field, weekend tailgate warriors strive for excellence and the accolades of their fans. They're always on the hunt for that recipe that's going to capture the taste buds of the crowd in a way that leaves them forever wanting more. If any of the above sounds like you, then you have found your spirit animal of a cookbook.

As a female tailgater, cook, and entertainer, I can tell you that most tailgate cookbooks don't really appeal to me or to my female tailgate friends. The ideas out there depict "sportsy" gridiron recipes that are focused on grilling, or they tend to be consistent with typical tailgate food. For example,

beer-can chicken. How "guy" is beer-can chicken? I mean, an open can of beer in the cavity of a chicken. Just so you know, in this book, you will not find anything as funky as beer-can chicken. Chicken and Waffle Cupcakes, yes, for sure, because they are as adorable as they are delicious. But sorry, kids—even if it is the moistest beer-infused chicken ever to be, there will be no cans of beer in a chicken here.

This book is dedicated to all you peeps out there who love to entertain surrounding game day and are looking for inspired ideas for tailgate entertaining. It's for those of you who have a need to elevate your tailgate entertaining with delicious, fun, and stylish food and decor—I get you! As competitive as the guys are at the grill, anyone who contributes to every other bite at the party is equally as focused on "bringing it"! Going big or going home rules the tailgate entertaining mentality. The steps you take to be organized and step up to game-changing fun food, the closer you get to tailgate glory! Go for it!

Why are we soooo excited about tailgate food? Because tailgate food is FUN food with a capital FUN. It is steeped in local tradition, made from the heart, and offered with pride. In this cookbook, you'll find decadent dishes you'll be proud to share. The recipes in this book don't shy away from the idea that the cheesier, the spicier, and the richer the dish is, the better! Check out the Roasted Corn, Bacon & Chipotle Dip. Oh, and there's the Donut and Cupcake Bar. I know, I know—donuts and cupcakes, displayed real pretty and in vast quantity. I accept that this is brilliant . . . and you're welcome.

Don't worry, I've got you covered on the social side too. I know you want the pics for social—that's why many of the recipes in the book are Instagram- and Pinterest-worthy. Tailgate fun food is so perfect for the camera. You'll also find vegan and vegetarian bites and recipes that are not tied to traditional tailgate food at all. Isn't that some innovative tailgate action? Yes, it is!

If you agree that tailgate entertaining goes way beyond beers in the cooler and a bag of chips opened alongside a big piece of grilled meat, this book will speak to you. If you add style to everything you do—if you don't scoff at red carpets, chandeliers, and the good china being an essential element of your game-day decor—you have found your home. You are the warrior of the party, the MVP of the next generation of leveled-up tailgating. Wear that badge as proud as you wear your team's colors. Because although it is full of deliciousness, game-day food doesn't just sate hunger, it also represents camaraderie of friendships bonded by team spirit. Sharing that kind of love for community and team is one of life's biggest touchdowns. Game-day food celebrates tried-and-true nostalgic dishes, heightening and satisfying the love for the tailgate experience. The team may bring the community to the tailgate, but food and drink keep the crowds coming back. Now get out there and tailgate your pretty face off! Whoot!

#TailgateFoodIsFunFood! #GoTeamTailgate! #WelcomeToTheTailgateRevolution! #BeATailgateLegend

CHAPTER 1
TAILGATE GLORY

Tailgating is as American as football. Let's hear it for the awesomeness of that! To party in the parking lot or set up a festive event in your living room or backyard around the game on the big screen is an American phenomenon unique to the US, something you won't find in any form in other countries around the world. This is all ours, people! Let's celebrate and tailgate in style! That's exactly what *The Tailgate Cookbook* does: it celebrates all of the diehard, inventive ways tailgate fans light it up on game day and the ways to bring tailgating to new heights with great food that makes each region of our country's food shine. The food that we create for our game-day grub is authentically influenced by the regions around the country, and many of the recipes in this book, although built with a whole lot of fun in mind, underscore the uniqueness of regional gridiron bites, as well as the fun traditions that go along with it all. For everyone who thinks that community-building food experiences are all about family meals, holiday dinners, or maybe a festival of some sort, I have one word: *tailgating*.

How dedicated are we to our tailgate revelry? Well, let me tell ya . . . It all begins in the off-season. While the snow flies, and spring moves into summer, and the basics of life take our time. While life is happening in the off-season, big tailgate plans are being made behind the scenes. Enthusiasts are quietly pushing closer toward epic days in the fall. They plot and plan all off-season for our most favorite season of the year . . . You guessed it, football season! January through July, fans all over this country hold on to their glory-day tailgate moments and begin to dust off their coolers and methodically organize for the happiest time of the year. Preparing for the weeks over weeks of collaborative menus and tailgate parties, working like champions to amp up their epic events. Emails fly through the interwebz bringing fellow fans together again for another season of over-the-top football worship.

What motivates us tailgate types to go to such lengths? Rooting for our team is priority number one, but tied to our love for our team is our motivation from memories of the amazing tailgate events and the "eats" that go along with it. Yes, that tasty, tasty tailgate food. Every weekend all football season long, homemade tailgate fun food gets served by generous friends in team-adorned tent cities all across the country. For football fans, the beginning of the season holds such hope for their team and a big appetite for all the season has to offer, all of it built on passion. The food, most definitely, is central to it all.

Tailgate history for the win! I want to help make you a more well-rounded tailgater, so, here are a few conversation starters for game day. When the heck did people start tailgating?

Tailgating prior to a football game is a tradition that's more than a century old, and just like it is now, tailgating began as a way to eat, drink, and be a community over sports before the game, during the game, and, for the diehards, after the game. That's why I don't find it surprising that as many as 45 percent of tailgaters never attend the game inside the stadium. I get this. I would likely be one of the 45 percent. I'm there for the party, for the food, and for the friends. That's exactly how tailgating got started. Food, friends, and . . . communities supporting their "home" team. Experts link the term "tailgating" to the First Battle of Bull Run

in 1861. It was the US Civil War's first major battle, and voyeurs traveled from DC to Manassas, Virginia, to cheer on their team, Union or Confederate, but before the battle came the picnic. Most of the people actually stayed to watched that game, likely in horror and . . . I think we all know who won. Historians also found that one of the next accounts of true football tailgating came before the first Rutgers vs Princeton games, where they grilled sausages in the field near the stadium 1869 style . . . with horses' tails as the "tail" part. Can't make this stuff up.

The more things change, the more they stay the same. Over the years, the sausage grilling continues, but now there are pickup trucks and SUVs to tailgate behind. If you stroll through any pregame stadium parking lot, you'll see feasts of more than just sausages over coals. You'll find an elevated food experience. Prime meats, a plethora of dips, and charcuterie boards with 1,000 varieties of handmade sausages paired with artisanal cheeses. Yes, we have evolved in our tailgating, but one thing that remains is our love for team and community, and those, in my opinion, are some of the best reasons to tailgate!

THE TAILGATE LIFE

Let's plan for months, spend thousands on gear, food, and beverages and then, starting in August, let's get up really early on Saturday and Sunday, no matter the weather, to host a DIY party in a parking lot. That, plus lots and lots of passion is the tailgate life. I would say that takes something called passion to drive folks to be up for all of that. That pounding heart most certainly lives and breathes in tailgating and is the first thing that hits you as you step foot in a stadium parking lot party. The beating drums of the marching band, the baton twirls, the sea of team color, the haze of sweet, smoky BBQ, and, of course, the team-spirit-laden smiling faces. Not to mention the idyllic backdrop of a sunny, crisp fall day. Those tailgate days begin with confident hope for a victory; surely the day will unfold with happy memory-making moments. Passion for football, the team, the food. It drives the entire tailgate experience.

Like sports, good food is best experienced live and in real time. Tailgating brings the two together for people who are living passionately devoted to both in that moment. Sports fans love tailgating because its comforts are similar to food's ability to bring people together, giving a sense of community and connection in a disconnected world, an important thing that tailgating does really well. Football tailgating culture is different from region to region around the country; each one is uniquely its own, but at the base of it all is love for team, community, and food.

Tailgating is a time to celebrate team, and people want to stand out with their celebrations. They want to show that they're the best fan in the parking lot and are going to be the best fan in the stadium.

One of the best parts of learning about tailgating culture is that it's not what most people probably think it is. People have the idea that tailgating is a drunken junk-food event. There's definitely that element to tailgating, but you'd be surprised by what the majority of tailgate culture and the tailgate lifestyle actually is.

After all of my travels to tailgates around the country, my mind was opened to a different aspect of tailgate life. What I saw was community, that tailgating was as much about family and community as it was about celebration. I also found that tailgates are multigenerational, with grandparents, parents, kids, and extended family—not just partying students. In many cases, diehard fans have attend a tailgate for forty-plus years, bringing their expected dish to share. I remember at the Ole Miss vs. LSU game a sweet southern grandma walked up with her pretty yellow cake carrier (with a stunning hummingbird cake inside) and a smile on her face. She gave me a hug to welcome me to their tailgate, and as she backed away, I noticed her sweatshirt said, "Go to Hell, Ole Miss." Ha!

Sweetest lady ever, bringing her prettiest cake to the party, but don't mess with her LSU. Just like her, week after week, season after season, fans diligently attend their tailgate. They may miss church on Sunday, but they don't miss their tailgate. Those bonds of the tailgate community sure are strong.

What should I wear? It's an "anything goes" situation. Fans wear giant hats, crazy wigs, and signed player jerseys. Some wear colorful costumes and paint their faces with team colors. One of my favorite team spirit trends is that tailgates have become fashion-forward events. Particularly in the south, ladies wear dresses made specifically for the event, all prettied-up in their team colors. Honestly, the best thing to wear is something that is comfortable, team spirit forward, and weather appropriate. Tank tops to flip flops to short skirts and sweatshirts. You do you, and you'll be perfectly outfitted for the party. Except guys in speedos. Strict rule on guys in thong bathing suits . . . Sorry, guys.

In that same vein, some regions host formal affairs, whereas other tailgates are all about team colors and gear.

Know your tailgate. There are things that you want to look up ahead of time before heading to the stadium. Most obvious is the weather forecast; tailgating in a downpour in the Northwest, a blizzard in Fargo, or any time in August and September in Texas requires special equipment.

Other gems: Know when the parking lot gates open. You don't want to show up an hour early and have to wait in your car. Know how much parking typically costs, and reserve your spot. It's worth bringing cash to pay for your spot because many parking lots only accept cash.

Also, know what the rules of that particular stadium are. In some cases, charcoal grills may be prohibited. What?! I know, horrible.

There may also be a glass ban. No glass bottles—only plastic cups on game day or you'll have to pay big fines.

Are our rivals our friends? It's a reality of the tailgate game. The fans from the other team will be tailgating in the same parking lot. It's time to rise above the rivalry and show the hospitality that your community is proud to share. I suggest disarming the other guys immediately with a bite and sip to kick things off right. Goodwill brings good vibes to your own team. Really, I promise that's how it works. It's a whole karma thing. A kill 'em with kindness kinda thing. Many times, tailgaters from other teams have traveled a great distance to cheer on their team, and we're all tailgating to have a good time, so it's important to respect everybody, regardless of team affiliation. All said, I'm not saying some good-natured trash talk is off the table. Represent!

What should I make? A few years back, I was lucky enough to be a recipe developer and brand talent for an ESPN-driven tailgate tour sponsored by Sam's Club and Coke Zero. I lived every football and tailgate lover's dream as a professional tailgater at more than twenty ESPN game days, attending some of the top college football tailgates around the US. Along the way, I ate lots of tasty tailgate food. I've had the privilege of being a guest of tailgates throughout the US. Although they are casual affairs, there was always a fancy flair. One of my favorite tailgates was put on by my tailgate friends at the University of South Carolina in Columbia, South Carolina. The Gourmet Gents tailgate crew, led by Chef Don, featured an unbelievable low-country boil that included seasoned boiled crab, potatoes, sausage, and corn. All of that coastal southern goodness was poured into a huge handmade boat. Yes, you read right: they made a boat, for that particular tailgate, to feature their amazing low-country boil. If that wasn't enough, they had ice sculptures, chandeliers, no fewer than two big screen TVs, and a huge custom-designed cake for dessert. There were blenders buzzing and pimento cheese mini sliders at the ready. The ladies were decked out in sundresses and heels in team colors. So what should you bring to a tailgate? Come on! You know I've got you covered with all the tasty tailgate grub. Dig into one of my recipe chapters and go team!

CHAPTER 2
TRAINING CAMP

Game-day conditioning that has you crushing nachos instead of two-a-day workouts? Sign me up!

Hey player, I'm standing here with my clipboard and whistle necklace ready to coach you on all things super haute and stylish tailgate! It's time to get serious, prepared, and really focused because tailgate teams are only as fun and organized as their pre-season planning. I sound intense, don't I? Well, if you're going for the glory, you have to have the stuff of a champion as you lead this thing, and there are some rules to the tailgate game. You can only win if you commit. Come on—I know you're hungry for victory, so let's do this!

The List. Make one list or five, whatever it takes—the almighty list will bring your tailgate to the next level, dare I say . . . your life. I'm a list-making superfan. As a veteran event planner, a football team mom, and an avid tailgate chef, my most important tool is a simple concept called "the list." As a list-maker from way back, when I

want things to be smooth and simple, list-making is my go-to super power. If you want to harness the powers of organization when planning a tailgate, you should take up the list-making habit, too. You will find three important lists here that will make your game day go off without a hitch. One of the first things always on my tailgate planning list is my core tailgate team contributors. First things first, make that list of your tailgate crew because many hands make light work, and it's just more fun to plan a tailgate with friends. Your next list, immediately following your crew list, is your food list! Yay! Because the food is what makes a tailgate worth doing.

The Menu—What's on the menu, and who's making what? Start planning your menu(s) by enlisting tailgate team members to handle specific elements of the food, or maybe, if you're super organized, plan and assign the menus for the whole season of tailgate gatherings. If you get this part organized right out of the gate, you'll enjoy weekend after awesome tailgate weekend of lots of fun, tasty, themed menus and that happy, all-hands-on-deck vibe. The tailgate menu is really where it all begins and everything else follows.

Here's a twist on tailgate entertaining . . . How about Homegating?—So, what the heck is this "homegating"?

Homegating is tailgating without the travel. Rock your family room, basement, garage, or back patio instead of loading up the gear. All the same rules apply. Still have folks pitch in on setup, food, and cleanup so that you can enjoy the party, too!

Have fun, because it's just tailgating—no need to stress! It's the journey AND the destination. Hopefully you see that even within the recipes and the "How Tos," tailgating is all about fun, and you should enjoy the planning, the execution of the dishes, and the event. You should be present and ready to have a blast at your tailgate! If you are not having fun in all of these steps, including at your tailgate/homegate, you're doing it wrong! No tough and crazy recipes should be attempted for tailgate noshing, unless, of course, you are going for tailgate chef glory—then, by all means, go for it! If you're looking to take your fellow revelers' breath away and raise your tailgate cred, check out the Chicken and Waffle Cupcakes, or maybe the super trendy and uber-cool-looking Sushi Donuts. Folks love them both because they are tasty with a gorgeous presentation, but both of these recipes have several steps and a bunch of ingredients. There are few of these

show-stopping recipes in the book that take some time. They are worth the work because they were created to impress with how they present and how delicious they are. I say go for it, but determine to enjoy the entire process, and then, added bonus, bask in the tailgate chef glory when people *oooh* and *ahhh* over your talent and that most fabulous treat at the tailgate.

Stress vs. Fun—Don't resent your tailgate! The main idea of a tailgate event is to bond with your fellow fans over food, drink, a few games of bags, and, of course, love of team. Just like there's "no crying in baseball," there's no stressing in tailgate entertaining. It's practically a tailgate law. There shall be no stressing, especially when creating tailgate grub. Stress out when you make your Thanksgiving dinner or when you host your boss. For those events, definitely make the highfalutin food, but for tailgating, it's all about flavor and fun mixed with some stylin' presentation to get the "wows." Fancy, sure, a little . . . Fun, absolutely, yes!

Substitutions and prepared foods are very welcome and, in fact, encouraged—don't be a hero and sacrifice your good time for the sake of making everything from scratch. Seriously, back away from a recipe with all raw ingredients. Subbing in is an awesome way to make recipes fast and delicious. Do it now, thank me later.

I give you permission to use ingredients that are already prepped by the grocery store, or even completely prepared by the grocery store. Yes, you heard me. This little ol' tailgate chef just said buy goodies and put them on pretty platters and display them in an awesome way, then . . . stay with me . . . call them your own! Wait—I mean, don't lie, but, you know, just set them out on some kind of gorgeous platter or bowl and step away. Not sure what I mean? No worries! I have you covered in the pages of this book.

Tailgating is a team sport. Delegation . . . ity-aty-ation! I don't like to see people not having fun at a tailgate party, especially the host. So, repeat after me: *I will NOT hog all the work . . . I will not singlehandedly make all the food, organize the tailgate, bring alllll the gear, invite all the people, etc. ALL BY MYSELF*, because . . . tailgating is a team sport, baby! That's what makes it so much fun! This coach is telling you to create one fabulous signature dish that gets all the accolades. Drop the mic, turn around, and mingle. A couple favorite words when it comes to tailgate or homegate cooking and hosting are "half-scratch" (made partially from scratch) and "grocery gourmet" (buying ready-made food and presenting it on pretty platters and bowls). Both of those are important to remember, along with my personal mantra—listen to me sing it . . . "De-le-gation! . . . ity-aty-ation!" (while clapping and chanting over and over). It's all about delegating!

So, in that spirit, delegate menu items to the team just like this: "Kelly, you make that killer Waldorf salad; please bring it to the tailgate on Saturday." Simple, right? Do that with five to seven more people and you've just taken tons off your plate. Why delegate so much? Because who wants to work that hard when there's fun to be had at the tailgate? It comes down to this: own your tailgate, enlist friends to help plan, get organized, don't stress, delegate all aspects of the tailgate, and no matter what, have fun!

THE TAILGATE COOKBOOK'S
OFFICIAL LIST OF TAILGATE CHECKLISTS

Don't make the rookie mistake of tailgating unprepared. To tailgate successfully, you need a game plan. Use these checklists to make sure you party like a pro.

Apps to help get your crew involved and organized!

Here are a few organizational apps that will be helpful with organizing your crew (or you can simply use Google Docs or an Excel spreadsheet and email).

- ThingToBring Event and Party Planner
- SignUpGenius
- Pro Party Planner

THE MENU ROSTER EXAMPLE
Tailgate Theme—Mexican
Week 1—Menu Sign-Up

- Flank Steak
- Guacamole
- Desserts
- Nachos
- Wings
- Coolers/Ice
- Salsa
- Side Dishes
- Drinks

TAILGATE MENU ACCOUTREMENTS
Squeeze bottles—they're great for mustard all the way through mayonnaise!

- Mustard
- Ketchup
- Mayo
- Pickle relish
- BBQ sauce

FOOD-RELATED PAPER GOODS
- Napkins
- Paper plates
- Paper towels
- Tablecloths
- Wet Wipes
- Plastic cups
- Plenty of garbage bags and a standing garbage bin
- Tongs and other utensils

ESSENTIALS AND OTHER THINGS TO CONSIDER

- Knives and a cutting board
- Labeled coolers for food, water, and for beverages for kids and adults
- Team tumblers—Tervis tumblers are so functional for tailgating, and I love that you can get custom logos placed on the insulated walls of the tumbler. Have a set of these with your team's logo tucked inside. Superfan action right there! I love all things Tervis!
- Football or frisbee to toss around
- A few portable phone chargers
- Toilet paper, just in case the Porta Potties run out
- Blender—There are blenders that are made to work with alternative energy.
- Portable grill
- Propane gas or charcoal
- Matches or lighter
- Grilling utensils
- Aluminum foil
- Plastic containers for leftovers
- Portable fire bowl and firewood
- Ponchos
- Umbrellas
- Sunscreen
- First aid kit
- Blankets
- Antacid

PRO TIPS:

- Pack everything you can the night before.
- Make sure you arrive at least four hours before the game starts so you can have plenty of time to set up.
- Keep your car stocked with tailgating essentials throughout the season.

NOTES & REMINDERS:

NEXT-LEVEL TAILGATE DECOR

Pretty things to bring to sass up your tailgate—No need to be cumbersome, but it's great to have some festive items that amp up the atmosphere. This is where your style gets to elevate the tailgate, you tailgatin' jedi master.

- The big balloon—The big balloon or a large flag that identifies your tailgate location for your fellow tailgaters is an important way for everyone to find the best tailgate around! Fly your tailgate flag high!
- Folding chairs
- Tablecloths
- Vintage soda crates—They come with different-sized compartments that can hold all sorts of things.
- Banners, pompoms, pennants, etc.—Add some team spirit!
- Tables—At least one large six- to eight-foot-long table is great to have to serve as the tailgate table
- Team decor—Check etsy.com, your team's website or bookstore, or a local hobby shop like Michaels or Hobby Lobby for fun decor!
- Hay bales—These are great for use around the tailgate site as extra seating or small tables to set a cup and plate on. Plus, they add to the rustic decor.
- Crates—Rustic antique bottle crates and barrels work great on the buffet to give height to tablescapes.
- Wool throws—Woolen plaid throws or throws with your team's colors are great to hang from the back of the pick-up or SUV while you use the back of the vehicle as a table. Also, having extra on hand for later afternoon into evening tailgates is nice when the weather gets cool.
- Baskets and platters and pretty cloth napkins to line them with
- Ice sculptures of the team—This is something I saw in South Carolina. They used the base of the sculpture to cool cans of soda and bottled water. It was over the top but awesome too!
- A team-spirit cake—The same South Carolina team took the event to new heights with a custom-designed team cake made by a local bakery.

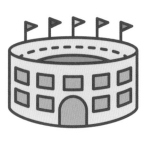

PRO TIP:
- Want to keep a cast-iron skillet of food warm without a chafer? Use three bricks to hold the skillet and place a sterno in the middle of the bricks. Not only does it keep the food warm, but it also looks great on a rustic tailgate table.

> *Cold-weather and warm-weather tailgating require special considerations. Here are some ways to keep food and people at the right temperature.*

THE COLD-WEATHER TAILGATE

- Blankets
- Hand and feet warmers—You can get these from your local drugstore.
- Mittens and hats
- Thermoses filled with soup, hot cocoa, coffee, and cider
- Fire pit (if the site allows)—Make sure to place it in a safe location within the event.
- Crockpots—They not only do the slow cook thing but are fantastic at holding food at a constant temperature.
- Chafers and sternos—These can also be used to keep things warm.

THE WARM-WEATHER TAILGATE

- Plenty of ice—Keeping things cold will be your biggest challenge.
- Separate coolers for food and drinks
- Separate coolers for kids' drinks and adult beverages
- Bowls that have a cooling system—There are bowls that have a water-based interior that can be chilled in the freezer and keep food cold for a long time.
- Tents and canopies—Use these to cover the food and keep it out of the sun. You can also bring mesh food nets to place on top of the food to help keep flies and other bugs from landing on it.
- Bungee cords, rope, and duct tape—You will need these to help safely secure the tents to the ground.
- Drink dispensers—Keep everyone hydrated by keeping ice-filled lemonade, sweet tea, and water in dispensers with spigots. This cuts costs and keeps the beverages in everyone's sight.
- Salt—No one likes a lukewarm drink. In a pinch, add salt to your ice for a faster chill.

PRO TIPS:

- In warm weather, think of tailgating as a "picnic." Pack food that doesn't require refrigeration at all times, like oil-based salads (mayonnaise goes bad quickly in warm weather), fruit, veggies, hummus, cheese, chips/crackers, etc.
- Don't pull food from the coolers until it is going to be eaten. Don't leave food out in the sun.
- Freeze your water bottles and place them in the cooler. They act as ice in the cooler and as they melt, they become ice-cold water for the crowd.

FOOD SAFETY

It's a thing. An important thing. Not to be a Debbie Downer, but . . . salmonella is gross and dangerous. Here are some tailgating food safety reminders:

- Have a food thermometer handy to temp your meats when they come off the grill.
- Be sure your burgers get heated to at least 160 degrees and your chicken reaches 165 degrees.
- Hand wipes, hand sanitizer, counter cleaner, serving utensils, gloves, and separate cutting boards for meat, bread, and raw produce are all a very good idea.
- Wash your hands in hot water with soap a lot when handling food or serving utensils—use gloves if you can.
- Sanitize tabletops, cutting surfaces, and utensils, including knives.

LET'S BE ACTIVE WHEN WE TAILGATE!

- Stereo and speakers
- Music (CDs, iPod, etc.)
- Frisbee
- Football
- Games (cornhole, ladder golf, etc.)
- Big screen and the big grills

PORTABLE POWER

- Before you plan the tailgate menu, you should consider how far your current power sources can take you.
- Can you manage with the gas or charcoal grill, or will you need further energy options?
- Alternatives for more amps include an electrical outlet where the power is sourced from your vehicle itself (through what used to be the cigarette lighter port) or a full-fledged gas generator.
- You may not think it's necessary, but if you are going to run a TV, computer, or blender, you probably need something to plug it into.

PRO TIP:
- Check with stadium rules and regulations on the type of fuel allowed on site. Some facilities might not allow open-flame grills, meaning no charcoal or wood pellets. That would mean some fast thinkin' on how to cook.

HOW TO PACK A COOLER

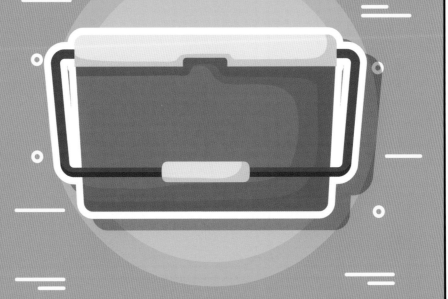

- Store your beverages in a different cooler from the meats, dairy products, and other perishables. The constant opening and closing of the cooler to get drinks allows warm air to enter and spoil food.

- Pack your meats into the cooler while they're still frozen to extend the length of time they can be kept cold.

- Try to completely fill the cooler and use ice or ice packs to fill any open spaces.

- Store items that you're going to use the most on top.

- Cold air travels downward—Put a layer of ice or cold packs on top of your food and drinks.

- Place a thermometer in each cooler to make sure they stay below 40 degrees Fahrenheit.

- Keep your coolers in the shade.

THE ULTIMATE
TAILGATE CHECKLIST

Tailgate Portable Grill
Propane / Charcoal
Gas Hose / Lighter Fluid
Lighters
Chairs
Folding Table
Coolers
Water
Ice /Frozen Bottled Water
First Aid Kit
Paper Towels
Tool Kit
Duct Tape / WD-40

GRILLING UTENSILS

Spatula
Tongs
Fork
Spoons
Knife (sharpened)
Cutting Board
Mixing Bowls
Grilling Mitts
BBQ Sauce Brush
Bottle Opener
Can Opener

Corkscrew
Skewers
Aluminum Foil
Aluminum Pans
Sauce Pan
Cooking Pot
Skillet
Meat Thermometer
Cooking Oil/Grilling Spray
Fire Extinguisher

FOOD ESSENTIALS

Main Course
Appetizers
Snacks / Chips
Desserts
Bacon!

FOODSTUFFS

Knives/Forks/Spoons
Red Solo Cups!
Cozies
Plates / Bowls
Tooth Picks

Napkins
Wet Wipes
Thermos
Gallon Freezer Bags

LIQUIDS

Drinking Water
Cleaning Water
Soda & Sport Drinks

CONDIMENTS

Spices!
Ketchup
Mustard
Mayonnaise
Salt & Pepper
BBQ Sauce
Relish
Chopped Onions
Pickles
Sauerkraut
Salsa / Dips
Butter

TAILGATING STAPLES

Team Flag, Pole & Holder
Canopy
Umbrellas
Generator
Extension Cords
Crock Pots
Blender / Bar Utensils
Rain Gear
Blankets
Portable Heater
Garbage Bags
Toilet Paper
Tailgate Games
A Football

MISCELLANEOUS ITEMS

Tickets!!!
Cell Phone / Charger
Camera
Binoculars
Sun Block
Mosquito Repellent
Sun Glasses
Jumper Cables

Spare Car Key
Flashlight & Lanterns
Bungee Cords
Extra Batteries
Driving Directions / Maps
Antacid / Aspirin
Sharpie Marker
Hat

NOTES & REMINDERS:

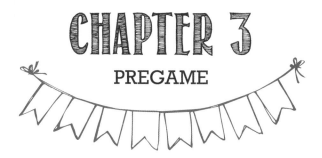

CHAPTER 3
PREGAME

Deviled Eggs, Dips, Wings

This chapter is the pregame of the pregame. I know—my mind is a little blown too. I'm actually really excited to share it with you because it's pretty special, filled with some truly new ideas for stylish and unique appetizers for tailgate eating. It's stacked with what could be, on its own, a complete tailgate. Not to invoke a Sophie's Choice moment and be forced to pick favorites or somehow pit siblings against each other, but it's definitely rivaling its other chapter brethren to be my favorite. From wings to double-dip-worthy dips to some exciting newcomers like the Sushi Donut and the Bloody Mary Jello Shot, this chapter has skills. Speaking of those newcomers, you are going to find serious tailgate food innovations within those newbies. Make one of those and out-genius everyone. As much as this chapter has in new ideas, it also celebrates some of the familiar, but of course, with a twist.

As I traveled the country, experiencing all of the diverse tailgates east, west, north, and south, one thing that was constant at every single tailgate was the omnipresent deviled egg. Seems basic enough, right? It's a simple dish that is presented with a perfectly piped decadent center or, if you are like me, scooped with a spoon. I like them either way, messy or precise. As you check out the six deviled egg recipes in this chapter, note that I give you both options. Because we eat with our eyes first, I attempt the piping, but I kind of bumble through it. I never seem to find the right tip for the piping bag (what happens to all of my piping tips?), so I end up using a plastic baggie, clipping the corner, and making a concerted attempt at pretty. Funny thing, I never get complaints. If the flavor is there, that's what matters most. You will find that the flavor is, indeed, there. Did you notice I said six deviled egg recipes? That's where the twists come in. It turns out the egg is incredible. Remember that ad campaign? The incredible edible egg . . . truer words have rarely been spoken. What are you waiting for? It's time to pregame the pregame, baby!

GRILLED CHICKEN WINGS WITH DR. BBQ'S ALABAMA WHITE SAUCE

Imagine having the enviable job of traveling the country for two football seasons and attending some of the top tailgate events around the country as a tailgate spokesperson. Then, imagine you get to do it with one of the authorities on barbeque. Lucky me, I got to do just that with my friend, Ray Lampe, Dr. BBQ. Here's a little bragging about my pal: he was inducted into the Barbeque Hall of Fame, is the spokesperson for the Big Green Egg, and has written over fifteen books about food over the years. He has appeared either as a judge or expert on most of the big food programs, including Food Network. He has truly had a fantastic career in food and food media. What's next for my friend? He's opened a new, highly acclaimed BBQ restaurant in the Tampa, Florida, area called none other than . . . Dr. BBQ's! Go check it out if you are in Tampa! I've learned so much about food, BBQ, and football from my friend, and I appreciate him sharing this iconic Dr. BBQ recipe with us all. I would try it if I were you. By the way, this Alabama White Sauce Wing . . . whoa, yum. He kinda knows what he's doing. Enjoy!

Makes 10 servings

Wings

10 fresh whole chicken wings

Dry rub, as needed

Dr. BBQ's Alabama White Sauce
   (recipe below)

Dr. BBQ's Alabama White Sauce

1 cup mayonnaise

⅓ cup white vinegar

2 Tbsp. prepared horseradish

1 Tbsp. freshly ground black pepper

1 Tbsp. sugar

Wings

1. With a sharp knife, cut the tips off of the chicken wings. Save the tips for stock. Slash the inside of the wing joint to help the wings cook more evenly, but don't cut them all the way through. Sprinkle liberally with dry rub.

2. Prepare the grill to cook the wings directly over medium heat. Grill the wings, turning often, for about 30 minutes. The wings are done when they are nicely browned and the juices run clear. Place the wings on a platter. You may serve the wings whole, but if you'd prefer to serve them in individual segments, cut them apart now.

3. In a small saucepan over medium heat, warm Dr. BBQ's Alabama White Sauce, stirring often, just until well blended. Transfer the wings to a large bowl. Pour the sauce over the wings. Toss to coat well.

4. Transfer to a platter to serve. Garnish with scallions sliced thinly on the bias.

Dr. BBQ's Alabama White Sauce

5. Combine all ingredients in a bowl, mix well, and refrigerate.

BUFFALO CAULIFLOWER NUGGETS

The bright color attracts, and the taste keeps them coming back. All the buffalo taste without all the chicken wing. Perfect for our vegan and vegetarian friends but a delicious treat for all. An easy appetizer or side dish for a movable feast.

Makes 6–8 servings

Buffalo Cauliflower Nuggets

1 large cauliflower, cut into florets

1 Tbsp. oil

salt and pepper to taste

½ cup butter (or vegan butter if desired)

½ cup hot sauce

1 tsp. granulated sugar

Vegan Dip

½ cup vegan mayonnaise

1 Tbsp. non-dairy milk

½ tsp. garlic powder

½ tsp. salt

½ tsp. onion powder

½ tsp. black pepper

1 Tbsp. fresh parsley

1 Tbsp. fresh lemon juice

1 cup apple cider vinegar

¼ tsp. fresh dill

salt and pepper to taste

For Serving

1. 15 celery sticks and 15 carrot sticks

Buffalo Cauliflower Nuggets

2. Place the cauliflower florets on a sheet pan and toss with the oil. Season with salt and pepper. Roast at 450 degrees until tender and slightly golden and charred.

3. Meanwhile, in a large saucepan over medium low heat, melt the butter and add the hot sauce. Stir until combined. Drizzle the butter and hot sauce mixture over the cauliflower. Place back in the oven to roast for another 10–15 minutes. Serve with Vegan Dip.

Vegan Dip

4. Blend all ingredients together. Chill for 30 minutes and serve. Add the celery and carrot sticks to the presentation for dipping.

GINGER STICKY CHICKEN DRUMMETTES

Drummettes versus wings is a personal preference, for sure. Although both have their advantages, at a tailgate, keeping one hand clean—available for plate/beverage holding, extra-sauce dipping, and possibly for some hand-shaking—is important. These drummettes get right to the point; they are super-meaty (no searching for the meat like you would on a wing), and they have their own built-in handle to help keep your hands sort of clean. When it comes to the rub and the sauce, these drummettes are slathered with some seriously intense flavor. Time-out . . . Did I mention a reduction of cola that gives the sauce a depth of sweet caramel flavor that brings this whole flavor profile together? Mix things up and surprise folks with something unexpected! Serve up this slightly spicy, Asian-inspired drummette instead of the same ol' chicken wing and be everyone's tailgate favorite. Believe me, no one is going to pass on this bangin' bite.

Makes 16–18 servings

Ginger Sticky Chicken Drumettes

16-18 fresh chicken drummettes

Ginger Rub (recipe included)

Spicy Sticky Sauce (recipe included)

Ginger Rub

1 tsp. ginger powder

1 tsp. garlic powder

1 tsp. salt

½ tsp. Chinese five spice

½ tsp. chili powder

¼ cup brown sugar

1 tsp. sesame oil

Spicy Sticky Sauce

½ cup soy sauce

½ tsp. soft brown sugar

2 (8-oz.) cans of your favorite
  cola, reduced to syrup
  (instructions below)

1 Tbsp. sesame oil

1 tsp. Chinese five spice

1 tsp. chili powder

a dash of salt

Ginger Sticky Chicken Drumettes

1. Pat the chicken drumsticks until they are dry to the touch. Place the drumettes in a large bowl and coat them with the Ginger Rub. Cover them and refrigerate for two hours.

2. Warm the grill to medium-high heat or preheat the oven to 450 degrees, depending on which form of cooking you choose.

To Grill the Drumettes

3. Grill the prepared drumettes on the grill for 20–25 minutes or until they have reached an internal temperature of 165 degrees, making sure to turn the chicken after 10–12 minutes. The chicken should easily pull from the grill at this point.

4. Once fully cooked, transfer the drumettes to the top rack of the grill for indirect heat. Brush the chicken with ¾ of the Spicy Sticky Sauce. Cover the grill and cook for just one minute. Quickly warm the reserved sauce before you pull the drumettes from the grill. Once the chicken is removed from the grill, pour the warm sauce over the drumettes and serve.

To Bake the Drumettes

5. Place the prepared drumettes on a parchment-lined sheet pan. Bake at 450 degrees for 25 minutes or until the internal temperature reaches 165 degrees, making sure to turn the chicken after 10–12 minutes.

6. Once fully cooked, brush the chicken with ¾ of the Spicy Sticky Sauce. Place the drumettes back in the oven for 3 minutes on broil. Quickly warm the reserved sauce before you pull the drumettes from the oven. Once the chicken is removed from the oven, pour the warm sauce over the drumettes. To transport to the tailgate, place the warm drumettes in small crockpot with a lid, or wrap them in foil and place them in a cooler. Depending how much time you have before serving, place the drumettes in the foil on a grill at the parking lot or field to warm.

7. Oh, and make sure to have some packets of wet napkins at the ready, because although tailgate eating is the perfect place for finger-lickin' food, fresh hands are needed for further noshing and glad-handing. Let's keep it clean, people!

Ginger Rub

8. Mix all ingredients together.

Spicy Sticky Sauce

9. In a medium pan, add the sauce ingredients. Stir the ingredients to incorporate and bring to a simmer, and then turn the heat to low. Reduce the mixture to about half, stirring throughout for 20–25 minutes. Reserve ¼ of the sauce for coating the drumettes after the initial cook phase.

THE BLOODY MARY JELL-O SHOT
alcohol free

There are things that seem to defy everything we are familiar with. Jell-O should be sweet and Bloody Marys should be savory, yet here we have it, all mixed up in this fun conversation starter. It's a wacky sounding Jell-O shot, but it actually works, and the presentation is gorgeous. The golden celery salt dust on the top of the shiny, savory Bloody Mary Jell-O not only enhances your presentation—it is 100% delicious. Flippin' the script on the average tailgate Jell-O shot!

makes 12 shots

12 large cherry tomatoes

4 oz. plain gelatin

1 cup boiling water

½ cup cold Bloody Mary mix

½ cup cold water

2 tsp. celery salt

1. Slice the top of the tomatoes off, and reserve the top for garnish. Seed the tomatoes and press the top rim of the tomato in a pile of celery salt.

2. Pour the gelatin into a large mixing bowl and add the boiling water. Continue stirring for two minutes or until the jello is completely dissolved. Add in the ½ cup of cold Bloody Mary Mix and ½ cup of cold water. Stir until mixed and pour into the cherry tomato cups, filling them almost all the way up.

3. Place the filled tomatoes in the refrigerator to set for 3 hours. Once set, sprinkle the top of the tomatoes with celery salt. Garnish with the reserved tomato top—it's like a little hat.

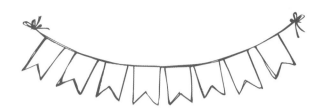

SHRIMP AND PEACH CEVICHE

This is a perfect warm-weather tailgate dish. Folks will love the cool, crisp taste and bright flavors with a kick of heat. The shrimp and avocado make this ceviche heartier than you may think. Serve this dish super chilled. Transport it covered in ice in a cooler. Ideally, serve the ceviche in an insulated, freezable bowl. In a pinch, place a regular serving bowl in a larger bowl filled with ice. Make sure that the serving bowl is tucked deep into the larger ice bowl and that the ice surrounds the sides of the serving bowl.

Makes 6–8 servings

1 lb. shrimp, uncooked, shelled, and deveined, cut into ½-inch pieces

juice of 1 orange

juice of 1 lemon

juice of 3 limes

1 red pepper, diced

½ tsp. red pepper flakes

1 jalapeño, seeded and diced

½ red onion, diced

¼ cup rice wine vinegar

2 Tbsp. sesame oil

2 fresh peaches, diced

2 avocados, peeled, pitted, and diced

6 Thai basil leaves, chiffonade

salt to taste

1 (12-oz.) bag plantain chips, for serving

1 head endive, for serving

1. Combine and toss all of the ingredients from the shrimp through the sesame oil in a large bowl. Cover the bowl with plastic wrap and refrigerate for 6–8 hours. The acids of the citrus and vinegar will "cook" the shrimp.

2. Remove the ceviche from the refrigerator and gently fold in the remaining ingredients. Cover the bowl and refrigerate for 30 minutes. Serve with plantain chips and endive leaves for scooping up the ceviche.

SUSHI DONUTS

Looking for a trendy conversation starter, something that everyone will fawn over? Something that will make them call you a tailgate chef genius? Check out the Sushi Donut! It's all the rage. Why make this for a tailgate? Because it's so not a typical tailgate dish. Did I mention that it's really fun looking? It's like a piece of art for your mouth! There is no real cooking, except the rice, but be sure to sharpen your knives because there will be slicing and chopping and plenty of prep and assembly. It will all be worth the work because you are an artist and the tailgate gives your art a place to be seen—oh, and . . . gobbled up! **Itadakimasu!**

Makes 6-8 servings

Sushi Donuts

sashimi-grade fish, thinly sliced

nori sheets, rounds and squares

soy sauce

wasabi

pickled ginger

cucumber, thinly sliced

radishes, thinly sliced

fish roe

avocado, thinly sliced

sesame seeds

black sesame seeds

Sushi Rice (recipe below)

Avocado Cream (recipe below)

Sushi Rice

⅔ cup rice wine vinegar

½ cup granulated sugar

2 tsp. salt

3 cups uncooked sushi rice or short-grain rice

3 cups water

Avocado Cream

1 avocado

4 oz. cream cheese, softened

1 Tbsp. lemon juice

2 tsp. wasabi

salt to taste

Sushi Donuts

1. Line a mini donut pan with plastic wrap. Next, lay your sushi toppings, veggies, and other accoutrements in the wells of the plastic-lined donut pan. Get creative, and use lots of colorful ingredients for each donut.

2. Next, press the rice into the well, filling it halfway. Then, snip the tip of the piping bag filled with the Avocado Cream and pipe the cream onto the rice. Top with more of the Sushi Rice until the well is completely full.

3. Lift the plastic wrap out of the donut pan. Gently pull the decorated donuts away from the plastic, revealing the Sushi Donuts. Top with a bit of the Avocado Cream. *Voila!* Sushi Donuts! I serve these in the donut pan, because this way they don't get damaged in transit.

Sushi Rice

4. In a medium pan, heat the rice wine vinegar with the sugar and salt. Mix until dissolved. Cook the sushi rice with the water in a thick-bottomed pot (or a rice cooker). Once your rice is cooked, transfer it to an uncovered bowl. Let it cool down to room temperature, but do not put it in the refrigerator.

Avocado Cream

5. In a medium bowl, use a mixer to mix the avocado, cream cheese, lemon juice, wasabi, and salt.

6. Fill a piping bag or gallon freezer bag for piping the avocado filling.

THE CLASSIC DEVILED EGG

This Classic Deviled Egg is truly steeped in history and tradition and can be found at almost every party table, fancy or casual. The taste is a built-in memory for most of us. Americans have a deep admiration for the classic deviled egg! A little sweet, a little savory, and a whole lot of wonderful. The deviled egg in all of its iterations is definitely a tailgate staple. As you move on through this chapter, you'll see my take on variations of this classic, but this base recipe remains one of the all-time favorites. #tradition

Makes 12 servings

6 large eggs

1 tsp. Dijon mustard

1-2 splashes Tabasco sauce or
   any other hot sauce you like

salt to taste

¼ tsp. freshly ground black pepper

½ tsp. pickle relish

3 Tbsp. mayonnaise

paprika, for garnish

chives, chopped, for garnish (optional)

1. Hard-boil the eggs according to the instructions below. Slice the eggs in half lengthwise from tip to end. Remove the egg yolks and reserve for filling.

2. Place the yolks in a medium bowl and mash with a fork. Add mustard, Tabasco, salt, pepper, and pickle relish. Stir in mayonnaise. Beat the mixture together until smooth. There will be chunks of relish.

3. Use a spoon or piping bag to fill each egg white with about 1½ teaspoons of the egg mixture. Then, dust the top of each egg with paprika. Garnish with chopped chives if desired.

WHO DOESN'T LOVE A DEVILED EGG? A standard at a tailgate party, for sure. Tailgates are known for taking things to the limit in flavor and fun and the next few recipes are a few variations on the *Classic Deviled Egg*, which, by itself is pretty fantastic. Don't miss the basics on "How to Boil an Egg" you think you know, and you probably do, but just in case, here's a little brush-up. Also, check out an innovative way to put a twist on the Classic Deviled Egg presentation. Let's call it the "Tailgate" cut. It helps keep the eggs from rolling about and a bit easier for transporting them.

HOW TO BOIL AN EGG 101

Getting back to the basics here. Place the eggs in a small saucepan. Cover them with cold water, place the pan over medium-high heat, and bring to a boil. Turn heat off. Cover and let sit for 10–12 minutes. Drain, and then rinse under cold water while peeling. Let them cool in the refrigerator for 15 minutes.

HOW TO CUT A DEVILED EGG
WITH FAB STYLE

Slice a very thin slice of egg off of each end of the egg to create a flat surface for the egg to sit on. Next, cut the eggs in half—not the long way from tip to end, but directly in half. Then carefully scoop out the yolks. Place the whites on a prep area. The eggs will have a very different look from the typical deviled egg. This doesn't change the flavor but does make prep, travel, and biting this style so much easier and, in my opinion, more fun looking than your average deviled egg presentation.

The classic
XO

"LOBSTER ROLL" DEVILED EGG

Cue the seaside chirps of seagulls and sunshine. This wicked-good version of a deviled egg will bring you there. Chunky lobster-filled centers combined with the crunch of the panko add so much extra love. Created to satisfy those "go big or go home" moments, this coastal-inspired bite is best for when it's all on the line. Make sure to keep these beauties chilled prior to serving. For this special recipe, a travel carrier made specifically for a deviled egg transport will be worth the money.

Makes 12 servings

"Lobster Roll" Deviled Eggs

6 large eggs

6 oz. chopped cooked lobster meat

1 tsp. Dijon mustard

1 Tbsp. chopped shallot

2 Tbsp. mayonnaise

¼ tsp. Old Bay seafood seasoning

1 tsp. capers

1 Tbsp. chives

¼ cup Panko Breadcrumb "Lobster Roll" Mixture (see instructions below; use 1 Tbsp. in Deviled Egg Mixture; reserve the rest for garnish)

Panko Breadcrumb "Lobster Roll" Mixture

½ cup panko breadcrumbs

2 Tbsp. Old Bay seasoning

1 Tbsp. melted butter

¼ tsp. Dijon mustard

1. Prepare the eggs according to the instructions on page 38.

"Lobster Roll" Deviled Eggs

2. In a medium bowl, mash 6 hardboiled egg yolks. Gently mix in all of the remaining ingredients for the Deviled Egg Mixture except for the chives. Brush the top surfaces and insides of the prepared egg whites with a light spread of mayonnaise, and then dip the top of the egg white in the panko mixture, coating the top surface of the egg. Next, spoon the Deviled Egg Mixture into the egg whites. Sprinkle the reserved chives to garnish the top of each filled egg.

Panko Breadcrumb "Lobster Roll" Mixture

3. Mix all of the ingredients for the Panko Breadcrumb "Lobster Roll" Mixture in a medium bowl. Spread the ingredients evenly onto a small parchment-lined sheet pan. Crisp the mixture in the oven for 5–7 minutes at 425 degrees. Let it cool.

CHIPOTLE CILANTRO DEVILED EGG

The traditional deviled egg meets the Southwest. Warning, this has a deep, smoky flavor but also has a bit of heat that hits a little late. Make sure you remove the seeds from the chipotle peppers to keep the heat to a mild-medium instead of caliente, unless you like and want caliente—then leave the seeds in the peppers. If you really want to back off of heat, use just the adobo sauce in the recipe and leave the peppers out.

Makes 24 deviled eggs (10–12 servings)

12 large eggs

½ cup mayonnaise

2 Tbsp. chipotle chilies in adobo sauce, peppers seeded and finely chopped

¼ cup fresh cilantro, finely chopped

1 tsp. Dijon mustard

2 Tbsp. pickled jalapeño, minced

salt and pepper to taste

1 tsp. hot smoked paprika, for garnish

1 Tbsp. pickled jalapeño, minced, for garnish

1 Tbsp. pimentos, minced, for garnish

24 fresh cilantro leaves, for garnish

1. Prepare the eggs according to the instructions on page 38.

2. Place the egg yolks, mayonnaise, chilies, cilantro, and mustard in a food processor; pulse until pureed. Stir in the minced jalapeño by hand and add salt and pepper as desired. Place the egg mixture in a piping bag. Place the filled piping bag in the refrigerator for 30 minutes to chill before piping.

3. Pipe or spoon-fill each egg. Garnish the eggs with a sprinkling of paprika, a couple pieces of jalapeño and pimento, and one cilantro leaf.

FIRE-ROASTED JALAPEÑO DEVILED EGG

Lasso a deviled egg and be right with the tailgate! This recipe puts the classic deviled egg in a corner. A nice, mellow char essence rules taste buds in this twist on tradition. Smoky, earthy flavors are all combined in what is basically a southwestern egg salad tucked in a two-bite flavor bomb. Giddy up!

Makes 8–10 servings (20 deviled eggs)

12 large eggs *

2 cups shredded Mexican-blend cheese

½ cup mayonnaise

½ tsp. Dijon mustard

¼ tsp. garlic powder

¼ tsp. ground cayenne pepper

¼ tsp. onion powder

salt and pepper to taste

2 Char-Roasted Jalapeños (instructions below)

½ bunch fresh cilantro, finely chopped; reserve an additional 20 small sprigs of cilantro from the bunch for garnish

1 jalapeño pepper, seeded, thinly sliced, and caramelized, for garnish

20 small pieces of jarred pimento or slivers of red pepper, for garnish (optional)

*2 full hardboiled eggs and 3 yolks from the remaining boiled eggs will be used in the filling; you can discard the remaining yolks or use them in other recipe.

1. Hard-boil the eggs according to the instructions on page 38. Follow the instructions for **How to Cut a Deviled Egg with Fab Style** (also provided on page 38) for 10 of the eggs. Set the remaining two whole eggs aside.

2. Chop the two whole hardboiled eggs into ¼ inch pieces and smash 3 additional yolks. Add to a mixing bowl. Next, add the remaining ingredients from the cheese through the ½ bunch of cilantro. Use the paddle attachment on your mixer to blend the mixture on low for 1 minute or until incorporated.

3. Using a spoon, scoop about 1½ teaspoons of the mixture into each egg, overfilling the egg. The texture of this mixture is chunky and will not pipe easily, so it's better to use a spoon to fill the egg whites. Then, garnish each egg with the reserved cilantro sprigs, slices of caramelized jalapeño peppers, and optional pimento bits or red pepper slivers.

Char-Roasted Jalapeño

4. Place the jalapeños directly on a grill or open flame for 5 minutes, turning frequently, until the outer skin of the pepper is blistered and charred. Immediately place the charred peppers into a plastic bag for about 3 minutes to steam off the charred skin. Peel much of the charred skin but leave some of the char on the pepper to add a charred flavor to the egg mixture. Seed and mince the pepper prior to adding it to the deviled egg mixture.

Fire Roasted
- Jalapeno -

THE DEVILED BACON

Oh my, how do you explain The Deviled Bacon? It's just so good! People are actually speechless after a bite of this crunchy, bacon-filled bite. Fans smile and hum a happy little song when they see these beauties comin' at 'em! No eggs-aggeration . . . They're that awesome! Somebody better check, because I think this game-day phenom was nominated for induction in the Football-Tailgate Hall of Fame—Sound unreal? Don't underestimate the power of bacon!

Makes 8–10 servings (12 deviled eggs)
You should probably make more, though.

6 large eggs

1½ lbs. bacon, cooked until crispy, divided–¾ lb. roughly chopped, ¾ lb. crispy (almost burnt) and broken into ½-inch shards

1 tsp. Dijon mustard

1-2 splashes Tabasco sauce or any other hot sauce you like

salt to taste

¼ tsp. freshly ground black pepper

¼ tsp. brown sugar, plus a small amount for garnish

3 Tbsp. mayonnaise

paprika, for garnish

1 Tbsp. chives, minced

1. Prepare the eggs according to the instructions on page 38.

2. Place roughly chopped bacon in a food processor and grind to a medium-fine texture. Add the yolks in the processor with the bacon. Add the mustard, Tabasco, salt, pepper, and brown sugar. Pulse a few times until completely incorporated. Next, stir the mayonnaise in gently until all ingredients are blended together.

3. Use a spoon or piping bag to fill each egg white with about 1½ teaspoons of the egg mixture. Then, dust the top of each egg with just a little paprika and a sprinkle of brown sugar. Garnish each generously with large shards of bacon. Yep, just stick those shards right in the egg mixture. Then, for a little color and fresh flavor, add a sprinkle of minced chives on each egg for the final garnish. Not only is it fun looking, that bacon crunch makes everyone squeal for more. Once you've set The Deviled Bacon out, make sure to stand far back from the dish and watch your tailgate crew come running! They can be such little piggies!

The Deviled Bacon

- The down South -
Pimento Cheese

THE DOWN SOUTH PIMENTO CHEESE & JALAPEÑO DEVILED EGG

Hey, y'all! Let's put a little South in your mouth! This recipe pays delicious homage to deep south tastebuds with the blended action of two stellar southern tailgate food favorites. Bringing together the best combination of the gentile deviled egg loaded with a hearty and decadent pimento cheese. This flavor packed bite gets ramped up with a crispy slice of caramelized jalapeno garnish. It adds a lot to make this deviled egg extra special. Make these ahead and secure them in in a specially made Deviled Egg container with compartments for each deviled egg. Pop this container in a cooler with ice or ice packs to keep temperature until ready to serve.

Makes 8–10 servings (20 deviled eggs)

10 large eggs

2 cups shredded extra-sharp cheddar cheese

1 (8-oz.) package cream cheese, softened

½ cup mayonnaise

¼ tsp. garlic powder

¼ tsp. ground cayenne pepper

¼ tsp. onion powder

1 jalapeño pepper, seeded, minced, and caramelized

4-ounce jar diced pimento, drained, 1 ounce reserved for garnish

salt and pepper to taste

paprika, for garnish

1 jalapeño pepper, seeded, thinly sliced, and caramelized, for garnish

1. Prepare the eggs according to the instructions on page 38.

2. Add 3 smashed yolks in a mixing bowl, and add remaining ingredients, except for garnish. Use the paddle attachment on your mixer to blend the mixture on low for 1 minute or until incorporated.

3. Use a spoon or piping bag to fill each egg white with about 1½ teaspoons of the egg mixture. Then, dust the top of each egg with a little paprika, and garnish them with the reserved pimento bits and slices of caramelized jalapeño pepper.

BLT DIP

The original triple threat, this dip has it all: bacon, lettuce, and the almighty tomato. Toast up some crusty bread, grill the romaine, grab a little grape tomato or crisp crackers, and dig in.

Makes 12–18 servings

BLT Dip

3 tomatoes, seeded and finely diced

1 lb. bacon, cooked and crisp, 9 slices crumbled (reserve remaining pieces for dipping)

½ cup mayonnaise

⅓ cup chopped green onion

½ cup minced parsley

¼ cup sour cream

½ cup shredded cheddar cheese

Grilled Romaine Lettuce, for dipping (instructions below)

1 loaf ciabatta bread, sliced in ½-inch thick slices, toasted, for dipping

1 pint grape tomatoes, for dipping

Grilled Romaine Lettuce

1 head romaine lettuce, sliced in half lengthwise

oil

salt and cracked pepper to taste

BLT Dip

1. In a large bowl, combine all of the BLT Dip ingredients except the Grilled Romaine Lettuce, bread, and grape tomatoes. Use a spatula to gently fold the ingredients together.

2. Cover and refrigerate for 1 hour to incorporate flavors, and then dip away!

Grilled Romaine Lettuce

3. Preheat grill to medium heat and lightly oil the grate. Drizzle olive oil over the romaine lettuce and sprinkle with kosher or sea salt and cracked pepper to taste. Place the lettuce cut-side down on preheated grill. Cook until the lettuce is slightly charred, 4–5 minutes.

GRILLED CORN, BACON, AND CHIPOTLE DIP

This is no run-of-the-mill dipping experience. Sure, there's the smoky essence of the bacon and chipotle, but the charred corn is the star of this dish, adding a pop of buttery, salty-sweet fire-roasted action. Make extra, because people will want more. Oh, and memorize this recipe, because folks will be asking for it often! Serve with your favorite tortilla chips or any other tasty crisp that can hold a hearty scoop of deliciousness.

Makes 8–10 servings (about 2½ cups)

2 ears corn, shucked

2 Tbsp. butter, melted

1 lb. bacon, cooked until crispy, diced

1 cup sour cream, softened

1 (8-oz.) package cream cheese, softened

¾ cup shredded Monterey Jack cheese

3 Tbsp. chipotle peppers with adobo sauce, peppers seeded and diced

2 Tbsp. fresh parsley, roughly chopped

2 Tbsp. smoked paprika

¾ cup shredded cheddar cheese

2 tsp. garlic powder

1 tsp. pepper

2 Tbsp. chopped chives

1. Heat grill to medium. Place the corn on the grill. Cover and cook for 10–15 minutes on direct heat, turning frequently, until the corn is charred on all sides. Let it cool.

2. Shave the kernels off of the corn into a medium-sized bowl. Add all of the remaining ingredients and gently fold until all ingredients are incorporated. Make this ahead and pop it in your cooler. Serve it, and watch people write in your name for MVP of the tailgate scene!

GRILLED ROMAINE LETTUCE WITH HEIRLOOM TOMATO AND ROASTED GARLIC VINAIGRETTE

Using this fresh vinaigrette over grilled romaine lettuce is super summery and perfect for a warm-weather tailgate party. The vinaigrette in this recipe is dippable and can also be used as a veggie dip or even a marinade. It's versatile and flavorful. It brightens any salad, veggie, or meat.

Makes 6-8 servings

Heirloom Tomato and Roasted Garlic Vinaigrette

2 vine-ripened red tomatoes, seeded

Roasted Garlic (instructions below)

2 Tbsp. red wine vinegar

2 Tbsp. extra virgin olive oil

3 Tbsp. grated Parmesan cheese, reserve 1 Tbsp. for garnish

2 Tbsp. fresh parsley or basil, finely chopped

salt and freshly ground pepper to taste

1 pint heirloom cherry tomatoes, diced

Grilled Romaine Lettuce (instructions below)

Roasted Garlic

3 garlic cloves

1 to 2 tsp. olive oil

salt to taste

Grilled Romaine Lettuce

1 head romaine lettuce, sliced lengthwise

oil

salt and cracked pepper to taste

Heirloom Tomato and Roasted Garlic Vinaigrette

1. Using a box grater over a bowl, grate the larger tomatoes. Press the Roasted Garlic out of its skin into the bowl. Whisk in the vinegar and drizzle the olive oil into the mixture.

2. Next, whip in the cheese, parsley, salt, and pepper. Add the cherry tomatoes into the vinaigrette and pour over the lettuce of choice (instructions for Grilled Romaine Lettuce below).

Roasted Garlic

3. Heat the oven to 400 degrees. Peel away the loose outer layers around a head of garlic. Leave the head itself intact with the cloves connected. Trim the top of the head of garlic about ⅛ inch to expose the tops of the garlic cloves.

4. Place in an oven safe bowl, drizzle 1–2 teaspoons of olive oil over the garlic, and sprinkle with kosher or sea salt. Roast the garlic in the oven for 30–40 minutes. Depending on the size and amount of garlic you are roasting, check the garlic after 20 minutes to see if it is golden brown and softened. If so, it's ready to use.

Grilled Romaine Lettuce

5. Preheat grill to medium heat and lightly oil the grate. Drizzle olive oil over the romaine lettuce and sprinkle with kosher or sea salt and cracked pepper to taste. Place the lettuce cut-side down on preheated grill. Cook until the lettuce is slightly charred, 4–5 minutes.

6. Drizzle with above vinaigrette and tomatoes and sprinkle with Parmesan cheese.

ROSEMARY & ROASTED GARLIC WHITE BEAN DIP

One of my all-time favorites. I could skip the veggies and just eat this with a spoon, and actually, I've been known to do it! This recipe is short on ingredients and tall on taste. The roasted garlic adds so much flavor to this creamy dip. In addition to veggies, I also add crostini, breadsticks, or sometimes pita chips to scoop. By the way, the drizzle of olive oil is important and adds a peppery bite. It's all just delicious.

Makes 6–8 servings

Rosemary & Roasted Garlic White Bean Dip

2 (16 oz.) cans white beans, drained (cannellini or northern white beans)

Roasted Garlic (instructions below)

1 lemon, zested and juiced

4 Tbsp. extra virgin olive oil, plus extra for drizzling

3-4 tsp. fresh rosemary, chopped, plus extra for garnish

flake sea salt and pepper to taste

1/8 tsp. red pepper flakes

Roasted Garlic

3 garlic cloves

1 to 2 tsp. olive oil

Rosemary & Roasted Garlic White Bean Dip

1. Add the drained beans, Roasted Garlic, lemon zest, and lemon juice to the bowl of a food processor. Process the mixture until smooth.

2. While the machine is running, drizzle the olive oil into the bowl. Add in the rosemary, salt, and pepper. Blend until combined.

3. Transfer the mixture to a bowl and refrigerate it for 20 minutes. Add a generous drizzle of olive oil to the top of the dip with a sprig of rosemary for a beautiful garnish, and serve.

4. For dipping, serve with an array of fresh vegetables, crostini, bread sticks, and pita chips.

Roasted Garlic

5. Heat the oven to 400 degrees. Peel away the loose outer layers around a head of garlic. Leave the head itself intact with the cloves connected. Trim the top of the head of garlic about 1/8 inch to expose the tops of the garlic cloves.

6. Place in an oven safe bowl and drizzle 1 to 2 teaspoons of olive oil over the garlic. Roast the garlic in the oven for 30–40 minutes. Depending on the size and amount of garlic you are roasting, check the garlic after 20 minutes to see if it is golden brown and softened. If so, it's ready to use.

SPICED CRAB

A bit of a mystery dip with bright flavors with a bold base that you just can't place. People just don't know what the special sauce is. Is it cardamom? No . . . Is it cinnamon? No . . . Is it clove? . . . No . . . Hmm, what is it? The Chinese five spice makes all the difference in creating a unique flavor profile that will have revelers coming back for more. If you don't have this spice in your collection, make this dip for an excuse to grab some. You'll use it more than you expect. It's the secret weapon of spices that people can't quite identify but really like.

Makes 10–12 servings

½ cup sour cream

2 Tbsp. mayonnaise

10 oz. cream cheese, softened

¼ cup pickled jalapeño, diced; reserve 5 or 6 thinly sliced jalapeños for garnish

1 Tbsp. fresh lemon juice

1 tsp. salt

¼ tsp. pepper

pinch of cayenne

½ Tbsp. Chinese five spice, reserve a sprinkle for garnish

1 (16-oz.) can lump crab

crispy wonton strips, for garnish

tortilla chips

1. In a medium bowl, add all of the ingredients from sour cream through Chinese five spice. Beat ingredients together with a hand mixer.

2. Drain crab and gently fold into mixture with a wooden spoon. Refrigerate for 1 hour.

3. Before serving, sprinkle the top of the dip with a Chinese five spice. Garnish with thinly sliced jalapeños and crispy wonton strips. Serve with tortilla chips.

THE 1950s' GREEN ONION DIP

This dip is easy as can be, and it's been a crowd pleaser since the 1950s, when my grandmother would make it for her parties. I don't think grandma ever tailgated, but I know she would approve of chip dippin' in one of our family's favorites at a tailgate or anywhere friends and family gather.

Makes 10–12 servings

½ small white onion

1 (8-oz.) package cream cheese, softened

3 Tbsp. whole milk

4 green onions with tops, minced,
 1 tsp. reserved for garnish

½ tsp. garlic powder

1. In a food processor, pulse the onion until a paste. In a small bowl, beat the cream cheese, milk, and onion paste until smooth. Stir in minced green onions and top with minced reserved green onions. Any chip will work well but I serve with this like my mom does to this day, with super crisp and salty kettle potato chips.

THE BIG, BAD SRIRACHA
FRIED CHICKPEA HUMMUS

A little crunch and a bit of heat take this hummus right out of the "ordinary ol' dip" range. Serve with a pretty array of grilled veggies, fresh crudités, or pita chips, and call it a "guilty pleasure." But even though it feels decadent, you have nothing to be guilty about.

Makes 6–8 servings

6 Tbsp. tahini

4 Tbsp. Sriracha, reserve 2 Tbsp. for drizzle

2 Tbsp. fresh lemon juice

2 (16-oz.) cans chickpeas, drained and patted dry, reserve half for frying

2 Tbsp. olive oil, reserve ½ Tbsp. for drizzle

salt and pepper to taste

½ tsp. white pepper

½ tsp. red pepper flakes

1 tsp. chopped parsley, for garnish

1. In a food processor, puree the tahini, Sriracha, and lemon juice with half of the chickpeas. Place the mixture in medium serving bowl.

2. Heat a small frying pan (not a nonstick pan) on medium-low heat. Add oil and heat to a ripple.

3. Fry the remaining chickpeas until golden brown, approximately 5 minutes. Sprinkle with salt and pepper. Top the hummus with the fried chickpeas, a drizzle of ½ tablespoon of olive oil, a sprinkle of red pepper flakes, a drizzle of Sriracha, and a dust of chopped parsley.

YO, IT'S PEPPERONI PIZZA DIP

Not the most glamorous of recipes, but sometimes sexy doesn't matter. Sometimes it's only about what's on the inside. So dig in, wayyy in, on this one. Don't miss one drippy, saucy, spicy, cheesy bite, because what may not be the Mona Lisa to your eyes is a pretty delicious picture to your taste buds.

Makes 10-12 servings

1 large loaf store-bought garlic bread, toasted

2 oz. pepperoni slices

3 cups shredded whole-milk mozzarella

1 (8 oz.) package cream cheese

1 cup part-skim ricotta cheese

½ cup finely grated Parmesan cheese

½ can tomato paste

4 garlic cloves, minced

1 tsp. kosher salt

1 tsp. dried oregano

1 tsp. red pepper flakes

2 large loaves store-bought garlic bread, toasted and sliced in ¼-inch planks, for dipping

1. Preheat the oven to 400 degrees.

2. Process one loaf of toasted garlic bread and 2 oz. of pepperoni slices together to a crumble. Press into bottom and up the sides of a 9-inch baking dish.

3. Put half of the mozzarella, half of the pepperoni, and all the remaining Pizza Mixture ingredients in a food processor. Process until smooth. Scoop the mixture over the crust crumble–filled 9-inch greased baking dish and sprinkle with the remaining mozzarella and pepperoni.

4. Bake in preheated oven for approximately 12 minutes or until the dip is bubbling and cheese is melted. Serve hot with planks of toasted garlic bread.

CHAPTER 4
SIDELINE ACTION

Nachos, the Super Char-"Cute"-rie, Mac Daddy Mac & Cheese

One of my favorite movies in the whole wide world is *Elf*. I know, *Elf* is hardly a tailgate inspiration, but in one of the scenes, Buddy the Elf is eating spaghetti with syrup. His new family asks him if he likes sugar. He enthusiastically lists the four main elf food groups: candy, candy canes, candy corns, and syrup. If I had to choose the four main food groups for tailgating, they would be wings, nachos, grilled meats, and bacon. In this chapter, and pretty much laced through the entire book, you'll find that I adhere to the main tailgate food groups in a dedicated way. You will also find a full Char-"Cute"-rie spread (Did I spell that wrong? Nope, read on.) with lots of tidbits of snacking inspiration and explanation. The word *charcuterie* intimidates people because it's kind of hard to say and seems super gourmet. It's a French word that describes any smoked, dry-cured, or cooked meat. Other cultures have their take on similar meat-driven displays. The Italians have what's called *salumi*, and the Germans call

it *delikatessen*. The meats, typically, are sausages, ham, bacon . . . lots of pork. This is all a perfect fit for tailgate party spreads, right?

In *The Tailgate Cookbook* I have founded a new version of the *charcuterie* . . . I have deemed the tailgate version to be called, the Char-"Cute"-rie. Let's spread the word and share this newest version of meat decadence with the world. I think this fun little twist on the old-world version of the *charcuterie* will be accepted worldwide as the new standard by which all meat-forward platters will be judged. The best part is that the Char-"Cute"-rie is an equal-opportunity buffet, letting other elements of deliciousness have their place. So let's do this thing! In addition to a ton of meaty snacks, there are nachos, guacamole, pizza, pretzels, cheesy dips, mustards, and other amazing recipes all propping up a new idea with a fun twist, *The Tailgate Cookbook's* very own Ultimate Tailgate Char-"Cute"-rie! I smell world domination here, people!

DIJON SLIDERS WITH CARAMELIZED ONIONS

I think sliders are an indicator of our tailgate-food revolution. We all want to sample all of the amazing dishes at a tailgate, and having to commit to a whole burger is just, frankly, too much. Sliders provide the perfect amount of burger to balance all of the other great food at the party. The best part is that sliders come in all sorts of flavors. This one will be a stand-out among the rest. It makes my mouth water thinking about this slider. It's just a cheeseburger with onions, but the Dijon ups the game. Not overstating things, this is a stellar food experience. Yum!

Makes 24 servings

Dijon Sliders with Caramelized Onions

2 lbs. 80/20 ground beef

¼ cup Dijon mustard

2 eggs, beaten

⅛ cup panko breadcrumbs

1 tsp. kosher salt

1 tsp. fresh cracked pepper

24 (2" × 2") slices Gruyere cheese

24 store-bought slider buns

Caramelized Onions (recipe below)

Caramelized Onions

2 Tbsp. butter

3 yellow onions, finely sliced

¼ cup chicken stock

½ Tbsp. kosher salt

½ Tbsp. sugar

Dijon Sliders with Caramelized Onions

1. Heat a 12- to 16-inch fry pan over medium heat. While it is heating, in a large bowl, gently fold together all the ingredients from ground beef through cracked pepper. Divide the mixture into 24 (2" × 2") patties. Place your patties half an inch apart in the fry pan. Do not crowd the pan (you will have to make the sliders in batches). Brown patties on both sides for 2 minutes for medium/medium-rare, longer for a more well-done burger.

2. Once you flip the burgers, place the cheese on the finished side to begin melting. If the cheese is not finished melting by the time the opposite side is finished browning, pull from heat and place a cover on the pan to speed melting. Once the cheese is melted, place the slider on a bun. Add a small dollop of Dijon mustard on top of the cheese and a small scoop of Caramelized Onions on top of the Dijon mustard. Place the top of the bun on the dressed burger. Eat. Swoon. Eat some more.

Caramelized Onions

3. Melt butter in a large, heavy-bottomed stainless steel or enameled cast-iron saucepan over high heat. Add onions and cook, stirring frequently, until bottom of saucepan has developed a brown fond (about 5 minutes). Add 2 tablespoons of chicken stock and scrape up the brown fond at the bottom of the pan. Repeat, adding chicken stock, reducing, and scraping, until onions are completely softened and deep brown. Season to taste with salt. Set aside to be used as a delicious top to the sliders.

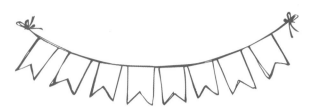

PIMENTO CHEESE JALAPEÑOS WRAPPED IN BACON

Keep your bacon-wrapped game strong, which is easy to do with these cuties. Everyone appreciates a plate of any combination of bacon, jalapeño, and pimento cheese pulled together in a tasty way. Here you have it!

Makes 50 servings

25 fresh jalapeño peppers

16 oz. chunky pimento cheese

2 lbs. bacon, each strip cut in half

1. Preheat the oven to 450 degrees.

2. Cut the peppers down the center lengthwise, from top just under the stem to bottom of the pepper. Then, slice the top of the pepper across below the stem area. You are cutting the stem almost off, creating a hinge where the top of the pepper opens not only lengthwise, it also opens up at the top of the pepper too. The top of the pepper is held on by just the hinge created on the back of the pepper. Keeping the stem and the top of the pepper attached is rustic and fun looking.

3. Remove seeds and pith from peppers. Make sure you use plastic gloves or wash your hands very carefully after working with the peppers. Your eyes and other parts will thank you. Be careful not to pull the top off or break the pepper. When done carefully, it looks great in the final presentation. Fill each pepper with pimento cheese.

4. Wrap half of a slice of bacon around each pepper. Place the peppers on baking sheets in the preheated oven for 10–15 minutes or until the bacon is fully cooked. Remove from oven and serve.

MAC DADDY MAC & CHEESE

They say that love comes in many forms. Is it weird to profess my "to-die-for" love for this dish? If it's wrong, I don't want to be right. Ti amo, formagio! No matter where you tailgate, this mac and cheese will be beloved. It has six melty cheeses that have almost designated this dish as its own special category within the food groups. You know, like if dairy is A, then this Mac Daddy Mac & Cheese is 1A. Don't miss the crispy Italian pancetta—Hubba hubba! Sexy Italian bacon alert! Go the extra mile and serve this dish warm, because a toasty scoop will make you everyone's amore. Keep this dish at temperature during travel by using an insulated cooler bag built to fit a casserole pan. The pan should stay warm through serving, keeping the dish at the right temperature for optimal lovin'.

Makes 6–8 servings

2 Tbsp. butter

1 onion, diced

10 oz. pancetta, diced

1 serrano pepper, seeded, roasted, and diced

1 pint (16 oz.) heavy cream

2 sprigs thyme

1 tsp. white pepper

1 cup shredded cheddar cheese

1 cup shredded Monterey Jack cheese

3 cups packaged four-cheese blend (usually Asiago, fontina, provolone, and Parmesan cheese)

¼ cup grated Parmesan cheese

2 roasted red peppers, seeded and sliced

2 Tbsp. chives, minced

16 oz. Campanelle-style pasta (a ruffled pasta that holds the cheese sauce. It's available at most grocery stores), cooked al dente for 9-12 minutes

¼ cup grated Parmesan cheese, for topping

1. Preheat the oven to 375 degrees.

2. Heat the butter at medium-high heat in a medium sauté pan. Add the diced onion and sauté 5–7 minutes or until softened.

3. In a 12-inch skillet, brown the pancetta evenly on medium-high heat for 5–7 minutes. Add the sautéed onions, roasted pepper, cream, thyme, and pepper to the pan. Bring the sauce to a simmer, 10–15 minutes. Stir with a wooden spoon, and reduce the sauce until it barely coats the back of the spoon, 10–15 minutes. Remove from heat. Discard the thyme sprigs.

4. Stir in the shredded cheeses. Once the cheeses have melted into the sauce, add the roasted red peppers. Add the cooked pasta and stir until well coated.

5. Pour pasta into a 9 x 13" buttered casserole dish. Top with ¼ cup of grated Parmesan cheese and bake until bubbly and slightly brown on the top, about 7 minutes. Pack it up and get ready to accept the accolades at the tailgate table. The people be like, "Oh. my. Gawd. This is sooooo good!" and you be like, "Oh, this ol' recipe?"

WARNING! RIDICULOUSLY ADDICTIVE BLUE CHEESE KETTLE CHIPS

Can't stop, won't stop. This blue-cheese sauced decadence will destroy all the other appetizers on the tailgate table. Even if someone says, "I'm really not a fan of blue cheese," even if they have a lactose intolerance, even if they aren't up for adding 20 lbs. to their backside, one bite and they will be hooked! Not kidding. It's something about that warm, creamy cheese sauce mixed with the crunch of the hard kettle chips and, oh yeah, the layers of bacon. Thank goodness for the freshness of the green onion throughout and as garnish to make you feel like at least you got a veggie in!

Makes 1–12 servings—depending on how willing you are to share this one.

3 Tbsp. butter

2 Tbsp. flour

2 cups heavy cream

⅛ tsp. black pepper

6 oz. blue cheese, small chunks at room temperature

1 (8 oz.) package cream cheese, softened

1 (10-oz.) bag of your favorite kettle chips

1 lb. crispy bacon, large crumbles

4 oz. blue cheese crumbles, for layering

1 bunch green onion, sliced

1. Preheat the oven to 450 degrees.

2. In a medium pan, melt the butter. Whisk the flour into the butter, and cook the mixture on medium heat for 1 minute. Add heavy cream and pepper. Continue cooking and stirring constantly for 5 minutes. Once at a thick consistency, turn heat to low and add blue cheese. Melt until it is fully incorporated. Remove from heat. Stir in cream cheese until incorporated into mixture.

To Serve:

3. Spread a layer of your favorite kettle chips in an oven-safe platter that has depth (sides). Generously layer with bacon crumbles, blue cheese crumbles, and green onions. Ladle the thick sauce over that initial layer and repeat. The last layer should be topped with a layer of bacon and blue cheese crumbles. Reserve the remaining green onion until after the sauce has been broiled. Broil for 4 minutes until the cheese is golden.

4. For garnish and a fresh flavor, sprinkle chopped green onions over the dish. Serve hot with additional chips (and maybe some forks). I suggest bringing this partially assembled to the tailgate. Finish assembly and place the dish on the grill for final warming of the fully assembled appetizer. When the dish sits, it can make the chips a little soggy, so transporting this dish fully sauced can be tricky, depending on timing.

THE CLASSIC HAM
AND SWISS SANDWICH

This is a tailgate staple and a fan favorite. The best thing to do is wrap them individually in tinfoil and place them in a small cooler. Set them aside at an afternoon tailgate. Go to the game. When you come out of the game, people will be hungry again. Pull these out of the cooler for a late-night, post-game tailgate snack. They will still be warm, and they will be very appreciated. Or simply leave them in the 9 x 13" pan you bake them in, and set it on the tailgate table.

Makes 12 servings

12 white dinner rolls, like King's Hawaiian

2 Tbsp. mustard, preferably spicy brown or Dijon

1 lb. Swiss cheese, sliced

12 pickle chips

1 lb. black forest ham, thinly sliced

4 oz. butter

2 shallots, minced

½ bunch parsley, minced

1. Preheat the oven to 350 degrees.

2. Slice the rolls in half using a serrated knife and arrange the bottom halves of the rolls in a large casserole dish. Add a layer of mustard, cheese, pickle, and then ham. Cover with the tops of the rolls.

3. In a small pan on low heat, melt the butter and sauté the shallots. Add the parsley, and remove from heat. Drizzle the sauce over the tops of the sandwiches. Bake the sandwiches in the preheated oven for 20–25 minutes or until the cheese is melted and the sandwiches are warmed through. Slice between the rolls to separate them, and serve them warm in the pan, or wrap each individually in tinfoil. Place individual sandwiches in a cooler to keep the sandwiches warm, at room temperature.

CHORIZO & BEAN SHEET-PAN NACHOS

A regular ground beef nacho is always excellent, a great choice. I have nothing bad to say at all about a regular nacho. I eat a platter whenever I get the chance. They are delicious. But every once in a while, mixing the nacho flavors up, throwing people off a little, testing their taste buds to see if they're on their game, is necessary. This variation on the typical ground-beef nacho is a gift to your crew. It will make them, and you, want to cheer! The corn, the beans, the Mexican chorizo . . . Surprises are at every turn on this nacho sheet pan! Make sure you get the Mexican chorizo, not the Spanish chorizo . . . or get the Spanish chorizo and not the Mexican chorizo. Actually, either will be great. Surprise!

Makes 10–12 servings

1 Tbsp. olive oil

2 garlic cloves, minced

1 cup corn kernels

1 lb. ground beef

2 Tbsp. cumin

1 lb. Mexican chorizo (or Spanish chorizo if desired)

24 oz. tortilla chips

1 (15-oz.) can black beans, warmed and drained

1 cup shredded cheddar cheese

½ cup shredded Monterey Jack cheese

1 pint cherry or grape tomatoes, sliced in half

½ head iceberg lettuce, shredded

¼ cup minced red onion

2 jalapeños, thinly sliced

3 Tbsp. sour cream

5 Tbsp. guacamole (see recipe on page 84)

2 Tbsp. fresh cilantro, chopped

1. Preheat the oven to 425 degrees.

2. In a skillet, warm the oil, and add the garlic. Sauté until translucent. Add the corn and cook until golden brown. Add the ground beef and the cumin. Cook on medium until the ground beef is browned and cooked through. Next, add the chorizo. Break it apart and brown it, incorporating it into the ground beef and corn.

3. Place 20 of the 24 ounces of chips on a parchment-lined large sheet pan. Spoon the prepared ground beef, chorizo, and corn mixture on the chips. Add black beans, and then add cheese evenly over the chips. Bake until cheese is fully melted (10–15 min). Remove from oven.

4. Place remaining chips over the melted sheet pan of nachos. Sprinkle tomatoes, lettuce, onion, and jalapeño slices on top. Spoon guacamole and sour cream on top of the warm nachos. Garnish with chopped cilantro.

CHUNKY CHILI NACHOS

Separately, chili and nachos are both staples at a tailgate, put the two together and you have something special! This recipe is full of all the best of both but live and die by how you layer the chips, cheese, and chili. Please note my specific instruction on layering. Following the layering pattern will make all the difference in minimizing the possibility of the dreaded soggy chip syndrome. Crispy chips matter.

Makes 10 servings

2 (18-oz.) bags of your favorite tortilla chips (1 bag for each sheet pan)

juice of 1 lime

sea salt to taste

36 oz. finely shredded cheddar and or Mexican blend finely shredded cheese

12 oz. refried beans, divided for topping on each sheet pan (see recipe on page 74)

6 cups Chunky Nacho Chili, divided for topping on each sheet pan (see recipe on page 75)

16 oz. guacamole, divided for topping on each sheet pan (see recipe on page 84)

16 oz. sour cream, divided for topping on each sheet pan

2 fresh jalapeños, thinly sliced

1 cup diced green onions, divided for topping on each sheet pan

1 pint cherry or grape tomatoes, halved, divided for topping on each sheet pan

16 oz. queso fresco, roughly cut into small crumbles

1 cup jalapeño-infused pickled onions, divided for topping on each sheet pan

1 cup chopped fresh cilantro, divided for topping on each sheet pan

1. Preheat the oven to 350 degrees

2. Spread your favorite tortilla chips on a parchment-lined sheet pan. Spritz lime juice over the chips. Sprinkle sea salt on top, and toast chips for 5 minutes in a 350-degree oven. Pull the chips out and sprinkle ½ cup of cheese on top and place back in the oven for 2 minutes. Do this before loading the nachos with accoutrements to start a strong nacho base.

3. Nachos are all about layering great ingredients that taste amazing together. Start by spreading the refried beans on the toasted cheesy chips, and then ladle the chunky chili onto the beans. Next, add the remaining shredded cheese. Pop this back in the oven for 4 minutes or until the cheese is melty. Once the cheese has melted, pull the chips out of the oven. Top with the guacamole and sour cream. Sprinkle with sliced jalapeño, green onions, tomatoes, and small chunks of queso fresco cheese. Top with fresh cilantro. Next . . . dig in!

EASY DELICIOUS
REFRIED BLACK BEANS

Toppings, toppings, toppings—that's what nachos are all about. Here's how you make one of the standard nacho accoutrements, the ever-so-flavorful refried black beans.

Makes enough to cover a sheet pan full of crispy nacho chips

2 Tbsp. olive or vegetable oil

½ cup finely chopped white onion

1 (16-oz.) can black beans, including liquid

1 medium garlic clove, pressed or finely minced

½ tsp. chili powder or cayenne pepper

salt to taste

1. Heat the oil in a medium-sized pan over medium-high heat. Add the onion and sauté until browned. Add the can of black beans, the garlic, and the chili powder.

2. Let the beans come to a high simmer, and then lower the heat to maintain a gentle simmer. Stir and mash until the beans are coarse and the mixture has thickened. Continue this process for 15–20 minutes. Add salt to taste. Scoop a large scoop warm from the pan onto your sheet-pan nachos.

CHUNKY NACHO CHILI

This is chili especially made for nachos. Why do you need a special chunky chili just for nachos? With nachos, you need a chunk factor that has a low ratio of saucey-ness. This chili is thick and chunky giving the chips more chunky crispy bites and less soggy chip action. No one likes soggy chip action. Can I get an Amen to that?! Go ahead, ladle this chili on your chips with confidence. Kick soggy chip out the door and get your crispy chunk on.

Makes 10–15 servings

2 lbs. ground beef, browned

2 (16-oz.) cans kidney beans, rinsed and drained

2 (16-oz.) cans black beans, rinsed and drained

2 (14½-oz.) cans diced tomatoes, drained

2 (10-oz.) cans diced tomatoes and green chilies, drained

1 (3-oz.) can chipotle in adobo

½ cup chopped cilantro

juice of 1 lime

1 large onion, chopped

1 medium green pepper, chopped

2 Tbsp. cumin

1 tsp. cayenne

1 tsp. salt

1 tsp. pepper

1. Place all of the ingredients in a 5-quart slow cooker. Turn it on high for two hours, and then turn it to medium-low for the remaining two hours of low and slow cooking.

KARI'S VEGAN LOADED NACHOS

No meat or cheese on my nachos, please. Say wha??? Awww . . . Step back. Take a taste. This alternate nacho loves you with all of its plant-based heart. Guess what? You're going to love it right back. If you met my friend Chef Kari Karch, you would see why. She is a chef that just happens to be vegan and specializes in clean eating. She's got our back as we work this whole vegan nacho thing out. She's a serious pro, so we are in good hands. Kari is the executive chef for Kenmore appliances and has her own vegan lifestyle website. Check it out at KariKarch.com for more of her great recipes and tips on healthy tailgating . . . I mean, living.

Makes 4 servings

3 cups riced cauliflower

1 Tbsp. olive oil

½ onion, minced

2 garlic cloves, minced

2 Tbsp. tomato paste

1 can chopped tomatoes, drained

1 Tbsp. liquid smoke

1 Tbsp. soy sauce

¼ cup of vegetable stock

2 Tbsp. cumin

1 tsp. ground coriander

2 Tbsp. chili powder

½ tsp. kosher salt

½ tsp. cracked black pepper

1 cup cashews, pulverized in food processor

3 cups tortilla chips

1 cup Vegan Queso (see recipe on page 80)

1 cup pico de gallo or salsa

½ cup prepared guacamole

3 green onions, diced

pickled jalapeños, for garnish

cilantro, for garnish

2 limes, quartered

1. Bring a large pot of water to a boil and add in the cauliflower. Cook for 4 minutes or until softened. Drain and set aside. In a large skillet, heat the olive oil over medium-high heat. Add in the onion, and cook for 3 minutes until translucent. Add in the garlic, and cook for an additional minute.

2. Add in the tomato paste, and stir. Cook the tomato paste with the mixture to deepen the flavor, about 1 minute. Add in the next 8 ingredients, from the chopped tomatoes through the cracked black pepper, and cook for 3 minutes. Stir in the vegetable stock and cashews. Let simmer for 10 minutes.

3. Adjust seasonings as needed and remove from heat. Set aside. In a large cast-iron skillet, add 2 handfuls of tortilla chips and spread evenly. Top with 2 large scoops of the cauliflower "meat," and then drizzle 3 tablespoons of the Vegan Queso on top. Top with pico de gallo, guacamole, green onions, pickled jalapenos, and cilantro. Serve with limes and lots of margaritas! Happy Eating!

MEXICAN BRAISED SHORT RIBS

This is the most important topping on the Mexican Braised Short Rib Sheet-Pan Nachos! Don't be lazy make this from scratch, I promise, it's worth it!

Makes 6–8 servings

1 tsp. ground cumin

1 tsp. smoked paprika

salt and pepper to taste

1½ lbs. short ribs, trimmed

Flour, for dusting of the short rib meat

1 Tbsp. olive oil

1 cup hot water

1 small red onion, diced

5 cloves of peeled garlic, minced

2 carrots, diced

1 (12-oz.) can crushed tomatoes

2½ cups beef stock

1. In a small bowl, combine cumin, paprika, salt, and pepper. Rub the mixture on the short ribs. Dust with flour, shaking off any excess.

2. In a skillet, heat oil. Caramelize the short ribs on all sides. Set aside.

3. Place in a bowl and pour hot water over them. Let steep until soft, 5–10 minutes.

4. In a dutch oven, add red onion, carrots, garlic, and crushed tomatoes. Place short ribs in next. Pour in beef stock. Cover and cook on low until the meat falls off the bones, 1½–2 hours.

5. Remove meat from the Crock-Pot. Strain liquid, reserving ¼ cup. Reduce the remaining liquid by half until it has thickened. While the liquid is reducing, shred the short ribs with two forks. Once the liquid is reduced, toss it with the shredded meat. Reserve ⅛ cup of liquid for the Easy and Delicious Refried Black Beans.

MEXICAN BRAISED SHORT RIB SHEET-PAN NACHOS

Whoa! This. Yes, this! It takes a little time for the low and slow braising of the short ribs but it's totally worth it. Everyone will love you for this one. The Horseradish Sour Cream with the Pickled Red Onions topping it all off is pure genius, if I say so, myself.

Makes 6–8 servings

1 (18-oz.) bag tortilla chips

juice of 1 lime

salt to taste

16 oz. finely shredded cheddar or Mexican-blend cheese

8 oz. cooked refried black beans

⅛ cup reserved braising liquid from short ribs

shredded Mexican Braised Short Rib meat (see recipe on page 78)

¼ cup Pickled Red Onions (see recipe on page 83)

1½ cups guacamole (see recipe on page 84)

1½ cups Horseradish Sour Cream (see recipe on page 81)

½ cup crumbled Cotija cheese

1. Preheat the oven to 350 degrees.

2. Spread your favorite store-bought tortilla chips on parchment-lined sheet pans (2 half-sized pans). Spritz lime juice over the nachos. Sprinkle sea salt on top, and toast chips for 5 minutes in the oven. Pull the chips out of the oven. Sprinkle ½ cup of cheese on the chips and place back in the oven for 2 minutes. Do this before loading the nachos with accoutrements to start a strong nacho base.

3. In a food processor, combine cooked black beans and the ⅛ cup of reserved braising liquid from the short ribs. You still want the black beans to be thick enough for spreading, so do not add too much liquid.

4. Spoon the black bean puree over the chips. Alternately layer the short ribs and black beans with layers of chips. Sprinkle with shredded Mexican cheese, and toast in the oven for 5 minutes to melt the cheese. Remove from the oven and add pickled red onion, a large scoop of guacamole, and a scoop of Horseradish Sour Cream. Top with small chunks of Cotija cheese.

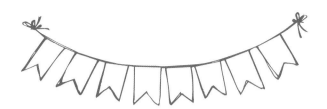

VEGAN QUESO

Serve as a yummie topping on your Vegan Nachos and/or just dive right in with a crisp corn chip!

Makes 4 servings

1 cup raw cashews, soaked for 8 hours and then drained

1 Tbsp. lemon juice

2 Tbsp. nutritional yeast

1 tsp. turmeric

½ cup salsa

1. In a high-powered blender, add all ingredients and puree for 3 minutes or until creamy. Adjust seasonings as needed and serve with nachos.

HORSERADISH SOUR CREAM

A topping to beat all toppings—creamy deliciousness with a depth of flavor that rivals all the deep flavors. Add a big scoop of this one to your Mexican Braised Short Rib Sheet-Pan Nachos! It goes great with the short ribs.

Makes 6–8 servings

3 oz. prepared horseradish

1 tsp. salt

1 tsp. black pepper

1 Tbsp. fresh minced garlic

8 oz. sour cream

1. In a small bowl, stir and incorporate together all ingredients. Refrigerate for ½ hour before scooping on top of the Mexican Braised Short Rib Sheet-Pan Nachos.

SERRANO SWEET PEPPER JELLY

Have you made jelly before? Don't be afraid—it is super easy and a cool thing to share at your tailgate on your very own Char-"Cute"-rie!

Makes 10 servings

6 serrano peppers, seeded and chopped (leave the seeds for more heat)

4–5 assorted colorful bell peppers, seeded and chopped

2 cups apple cider vinegar

2 cups sugar

1 cup honey

1 box no-sugar pectin

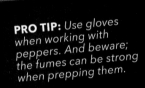

PRO TIP: *Use gloves when working with peppers. And beware; the fumes can be strong when prepping them.*

1. Wash the serrano peppers and trim the stem end off. Remove the seeds if you want a milder jelly. Roughly chop the peppers. Pulse them in the food processor until finely minced. Put the peppers into a large pot.

2. Wash and trim the bell peppers. Remove the seeds. Roughly chop the peppers. Pulse them in the food processor until finely minced. Add the bell peppers to the pot with the prepared serrano peppers.

3. Add the vinegar, honey and sugar. Bring to a boil. Next, add the pectin. Boil, stirring constantly, for one minute. Pour the hot liquid into clean jars. Set aside to cool. When the jelly is cool, cap and refrigerate the jars. The jelly will thicken as it cools.

PICKLED RED ONIONS

With all that deep depth of flavor in the braised meats and the creamy horseradish cream, you need a little bright, sour flavor to balance things. Pickled onions are pretty, delicious and easy to make. Pile them high on top of these epic nachos.

Makes 6–8 servings

2-3 cups water

1 medium red onion, sliced

1 garlic clove

½ tsp. sugar

½ tsp. salt

¾ cup rice vinegar, white vinegar, or apple cider vinegar

1. Start to boil 2–3 cups of water. Peel and thinly slice the onion into approximately ¼-inch moon-shaped slices. Peel the garlic clove, cut it in half, and smash it.

2. In a small bowl, add the sugar, salt, garlic, and vinegar. Stir to dissolve.

3. Place the onions in a strainer and slowly pour the boiling water over the onions. Let them drain. Add the onions to the bowl with the vinegar mixture and stir gently. Let sit and mingle for 1 hour prior to scooping the pickled onions out of the bowl and on top of the Mexican Braised Short Rib Sheet-Pan Nachos.

GUACAMOLE

This is a simple, yet delicious, chunky guac recipe, and it is excited to be used on all sorts of nacho sheet-pan recipes, or just enjoyed on its own.

Makes 8–10 servings

2 large ripe avocados, peeled, pitted, and diced

1 Tbsp. fresh lime juice

1 tsp. salt

⅛ tsp. chili powder or cayenne powder

1 medium tomato, seeded and chopped; reserve 2 Tbsp. for topping

1 clove garlic, finely chopped

2 Tbsp. finely chopped onion

1 tsp. fresh cilantro, chopped

1. In a large bowl, add avocados, lime juice, salt, and chili powder. Mash with fork. Gently stir in the tomato, garlic, and onion.

2. Sprinkle top with reserved tomato and cilantro. Place one giant scoop onto sheet-pan nachos, or scoop one awesome scoop at a time with a bag of nacho chips.

ELOTE GUACAMOLE WITH CILANTRO CREMA

What the heck is Elote? Deliciousness, that's what it is. Bright lime-enhanced cream, topped with corn on the cob, sprinkled with a fresh crumbled Chihuahua cheese and fresh cilantro. Using all the best of summer ingredients, this guacamole celebrates the delicious Elote with fresh, bright, and complex flavors. Serve with tortilla chips.

Makes 8–10 servings

Elote Guacamole with Cilantro Crema

3 ripe avocados, peeled, pitted, and diced

Grilled Corn (instructions below)

1 serrano chili, finely diced

1 small red onion, finely diced

juice of 1 lime

4 Tbsp. olive oil

¼ cup fresh cilantro, chopped

salt and pepper to taste

Cilantro Crema (recipe below)

Chihuahua cheese

1 bag tortilla chips, for scooping

Grilled Corn

4 fresh ears corn

1 Tbsp. salt

Cilantro Crema

½ cup fresh cilantro, chopped

¼ cup sour cream

3 Tbsp. mayonnaise

2 Tbsp. sliced green onions

1 tsp. grated lime rind

1½ tsp. fresh lime juice

2 cloves roasted garlic, minced (see instructions for roasting garlic on page 51)

salt to taste

Elote Guacamole with Cilantro Crema

1. Place the diced avocados in a medium bowl and mash into chunks with a fork. Add the Grilled Corn, serrano, onion, lime juice, oil, cilantro, salt, and pepper, and gently combine. Scoop a large dollop of Cilantro Crema on top of the Elote Guacamole. Sprinkle with a generous amount of Chihuahua cheese.

Grilled Corn

2. Heat the grill to medium. Pull back and tie the ends of the ears of corn together with kitchen string. Place the ears of corn in a large bowl of cold water with 1 tablespoon of salt for 7–10 minutes.

3. Remove corn from water. Place the corn on the grill, close the cover, and grill for 20 minutes, turning every 5 minutes or so. Cook until kernels are tender. Remove from grill and slice the kernels from the cob. To remove kernels from cob, stand cob upright on its stem end in a large bowl. Cut down the sides of cob with a sharp knife—don't cut into the cob. The grilled kernels are the base for the Elote.

Cilantro Crema

4. In a small bowl, stir in all of the ingredients. Whisk together. Scoop a generous mound on top of Elote Guacamole. Place the remaining Cilantro Crema to the side for additional scooping alongside the guac.

POMEGRANATE GUACAMOLE

The sweet, bright flavors in the pomegranate complement the bright citrus in the lime. All the flavors work together—the pomegranate gives a pop and crunch that makes this a really fun bite. Plus it's easy and pretty, too.

Makes 8-10 servings

2 medium ripe avocados, peeled, pitted, and diced

½ cup fresh cilantro, chopped

¼ cup diced red onion

juice of 1 lime

½ cup pomegranate seeds

salt and pepper to taste

tortilla chips or veggies, for scooping

1. In a large bowl, add the diced avocados, cilantro, onion, and lime juice. Mash together, leaving it a bit chunky. Stir in the pomegranate seeds, and then serve the guacamole with chips or assorted veggies.

PRO TIP: Keep the avocado pit in the guacamole until it is served.

ROASTED TOMATILLO GUACAMOLE

Did you know the tomatillo is part of the nightshade family? It's a nightshade veggie, whereas the tomato is nightshade fruit. It's the cousin of the tomato and . . . the gooseberry. Now how smart are you going to sound when serving this chunky salsa-like guacamole? Roasting the tomatillo adds a slight crunch. Getting a little char on the tomatillo brings out some great char flavor and tomatillo sweetness. When you bite into this guacamole, you have to ask yourself, which chunk is this going to be—tomatillo or avocado? Or maybe both!

Makes 10 servings

8 Roasted Tomatillos (instructions to the right)

1 cup fresh cilantro

1 avocado, peeled, pitted, peeled, and diced

½ onion, chopped

1 jalapeño, seeded and chopped

2 roasted garlic cloves (see instructions for roasting garlic on page 51)

juice of 1 lime

1½ tsp. ground cumin

salt and pepper to taste

oil, for drizzling over tomatillos before roasting

tortilla chips, for dipping

Roasted Tomatillo Guacamole

1. Blend the tomatillo into a thick, chunky salsa texture. In a medium bowl, combine the tomatillo and the remaining ingredients. Gently stir together—this should have a chunky texture. Chill for 30 minutes to incorporate flavors. Serve with tortilla chips.

Roasted Tomatillos

2. Preheat oven to broil. Peel the outer tomatillo skin. Rinse the tomatillos. Quarter the tomatillos and spread them on a sheet pan. Drizzle with oil and dust with salt. Broil until the skin is blistered.

CHEDDAR CHEESE DIP IN A BREAD BOWL

Grab a giant pretzel, dig in deep, and give it to a friend. That's what tailgating is all about, sharing passions. Okay, we may be going too far with sharing our cheese-dip-laden giant pretzels. To make transport to the tailgate with this bad boy mess-free, make this ahead, pour the dip in a large thermos for travel, and pull out the pretzels, the bread bowl, and the rest of the spread. Sit back and enjoy how cool it looks when friends dig in with your made-from-scratch giant pretzels.

Makes 10-15 servings

1 (8-oz.) package cream cheese, softened

2 cups cheddar cheese, reserve ½ cup for topping

1 cup grated white cheddar

1 cup grated mozzarella, reserve ½ cup for topping

1 tsp. cayenne

¼ cup water

3 dashes of hot sauce

2 Tbsp. chives, chopped

1 large football-shaped crusty bread bowl

* This must be a bread with a hard outer crust. Sourdough or an Italian old-world bread works well.

1. Preheat the oven to 350 degrees.

2. In a medium bowl, stir cream cheese until smooth. Add 1½ cups grated cheddar cheese, 1 cup grated white cheddar cheese, and ½ cup of the grated mozzarella. Stir to combine. Add the cayenne, water, and hot sauce. Stir until completely mixed.

3. Pour into a hollowed bread bowl. Sprinkle with remaining cheddar and mozzarella. Garnish with chives and set on your gorgeous Char-"Cute"-rie.

BACON & CHEDDAR SOFT PRETZELS WITH BACON MUSTARD DIP

You can just go buy soft pretzels at the grocery store, or you can have some fun and make these from scratch. If you are busy and can't quite get to the pretzels, just make the Bacon Mustard Dip and buy the pretzels. If you go for the entire recipe, make sure everyone knows that YOU made the pretzels and the mustard from SCRATCH! That should get some extra tailgate chef cred. Either way, have a blast at the party—that's what counts!

Makes 10 servings (10 soft pretzels)

Bacon & Cheddar Soft Pretzels

12 oz. water

¼ oz. active dry yeast

2 Tbsp. butter, melted

2 Tbsp. sugar

1½ tsp. salt

¼ lb. English cheddar, thick sliced

½ lb. cheddar, thick sliced

½ lb. crisp bacon crumbles

4½ cups flour

10 cups water

¾ cup baking soda

¼ Tbsp. caraway seeds

Egg Wash (instructions below)

coarse kosher salt, for topping

Bacon Mustard Dip (recipe below)

Egg Wash

1 large egg yolk

1 Tbsp. water

Bacon Mustard Dip

½ cup brown mustard seeds

½ cup apple cider vinegar

½ cup water

½ cup of dark ale

3 Tbsp. crushed crisp cooked bacon

3 Tbsp. light brown sugar

1 Tbsp. honey

½ tsp. salt

Bacon & Cheddar Soft Pretzels

1. Preheat the oven to 425 degrees.

2. In a medium saucepan, heat water to a simmer. Let simmer for 5 minutes. Remove from heat and let sit for 5 minutes. Stir in yeast until dissolved.

3. In a large bowl, combine butter, sugar, salt, yeast mixture, cheese, bacon, and 3 cups flour; beat on medium speed. On a floured surface, knead until pliable, 6–8 minutes. Place in a greased bowl, turning once to grease the entire ball. Cover with plastic wrap and let rise in a warm place until doubled for about an hour.

4. Punch dough down. Turn onto a lightly floured surface. Divide and shape into eight balls. Roll each into a 20-inch-long rope. Curve ends of each rope and twist into a pretzel shape. Pinch ends to seal the pretzel shape.

5. Bring water and baking soda to a boil in a large pot. Drop pretzels into boiling water. Cook 20–30 seconds. Remove and drain well.

6. Place boiled pretzels on parchment-lined baking sheet. Whisk Egg Wash ingredients together in a bowl and brush over pretzels. Sprinkle each pretzel with caraway seeds and salt. Bake 10 minutes or until golden brown. Serve with Bacon Mustard Dip.

Bacon Mustard Dip

7. In a medium bowl, stir mustard seeds, vinegar, and water together until combined. Cover the mixture with plastic wrap and set aside for 9–12 hours or until the liquid has been absorbed.

8. Stir the remaining ingredients into the mixture and spoon into a food processor. Pulse mixture 6– 8 times before stirring on medium for 25–50 seconds. Pour mixture into a bowl. Cover and refrigerate.

BUILD AN ULTIMATE TAILGATE CHAR-"CUTE"-RIE DISPLAY!

Coming single, get ready to mingle around the gorgeous and easy, char-Cute-rie

The Char-Cute-rie

You see what I did there? The whole "Cute" thing? Because this is not your typical charcuterie platter, this is an elevated tailgate play and that means, bringing style, flavors and fun! One main point that I'd like to make about the char-Cute-rie and charcuterie platters in general. They are one of my favorite things to do when entertaining, because, it's so super easy to do and packs a huge wow! punch. I have recipes that you can make for your platter but . . . come a little closer I have a secret . . . ready? Here goes . . . you can build an incredible char-Cute-rie without cooking One. Single. Thing. I'm telling you. No joke. You just need to know what goes on a char-Cute-rie and pick up fully created goodies at the grocery store, open containers, slice up some sausages, lay out some breads, etc. Or, like I've done on the char-Cute-rie here, include a bit of your own creations with some store-bought nosh. I mean, you don't want to actually cure meats, do you?

Check out the elements of the Ultimate Tailgate Char-Cute-rie!

Ultimate Tailgate Char-Cute-rie Decor

It begins with the tablescape. It's about layering and building. Lay down a colored tablecloth to start and begin to build by layering festive team-spirit decor, pendants, add a little burlap, a helmet, and old football, bright team colors, pom poms and rustic platters and baskets, a big picnic basket, cloth napkins, vintage pop crates. All of this is the base of the decor for your Ultimate Tailgate Char-Cute-rie. Just add awesome food and it's go time!

The Regular, Everyday Charcuterie

Something pre-sliced (thin cured meats), something that gets sliced (like cheese and hard meats), something spreadable, and accents (like olives, crackers, cheese, tapenade, jam, chutney, hummus, bread, mustard, seasonal fruit, and even a little honey).

Now, that's the formal version of what should be included in a charcuterie. It's very lovely, but we gotta tailgate-it up a bit.

Ultimate Tailgate Char-(super)-Cute-rie

A lot of grilled Sausages, stacked up next to some of the Bacon Mustard Dip (recipe included), and other awesome mustards, Bacon & Cheddar Soft Pretzels (recipe included), Serrano Sweet Pepper Jelly, a variety of hearty cheese chunks, olives stuffed with blue cheese, bread, tortilla chips, nuts, mini pizzas, corn nuts, jerky and . . . wait for it, grapes—boom, mic. drop.

This is how we do it!

Dazzle your tailgate crew and get your char-Cute-rie on!

CHAR-"CUTE"-RIECOMPONENTS

Something you slice
Cheese and hard meats

SomethingPre-Sliced
Thin cured meats

Beverages
All kinds of drinks

Accents
Bean or veggie-based spreads, soft cheese, jams, preserves, fruits, mustards, pickles, breads, crackers, seasonal items

Something Spreadable
Meat pates or vegetarian equivalents

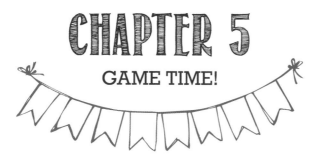

CHAPTER 5
GAME TIME!

The Hearty Bites

It may seem like the grilled meats are the only game in town when it comes to main-dish action at a tailgate, but there's so much more to consider. The center-plate items on game day are true comfort foods made with love. Asian noodle soups, big, thick, bacon-laden sandwiches, slow cookers stocked with warm, rich goodness. This is where satisfying big bites like a Buffalo Chicken Pizza and Cheeseburger live. Although comfort foods from around the country differ, the common thread is their hearty, belly-filling factor. The center-plate main dishes are as filling as they are delicious. Grab a big fork or a spoon . . . or maybe a spork. Either one of those works—just dig right in!

ADOBO LAMB POPS WITH A CHAR-ROASTED POBLANO DIPPING SAUCE

When I tested these, people licked the poblano dipping sauce bowl clean. I wish I was exaggerating, but I can only tell the truth. Someone, not naming names, actually licked the bowl. You've been warned; it's that powerful of a yum.

Makes 12 servings

Adobo Lamb Pops

12 individual lamb chops *

½ cup of your favorite BBQ rub

Chipotle Adobo Rub Paste (recipe below)

Poblano Lime Dipping Sauce, for serving

Chipotle Adobo Rub Paste

1 (24-oz.) can chipotle peppers in adobo sauce

¼ cup of your favorite BBQ rub

1 tsp. salt

Poblano Lime Dipping Sauce

4 poblanos, charred

2 cups plain Greek yogurt

juice of 1 lime

3 cloves roasted garlic (instructions below)

1½ tsp. salt

¼ tsp. black pepper

* Make sure the bone (the handle) has been cleaned up. You want the bone to be a clean handle for optimal tailgate eating. Also, score the backside of the ribs—there is a thin membrane that needs to be scored with a sharp knife on a diagonal repeatedly. An unscored membrane will make the chop tough to bite.

PRO TIP: The rub you use should be something smoky to match the flavors of the adobo and chipotle. I find that rubs are a personal preference; my advice, though, is to load it up with the rub initially and pack the paste on tight. These are extremely flavorful. The sauce cools down the spice. It's all deliciousness. The power of the roasted poblano is real.

Adobo Lamb Pops

1. Coat the chops with ½ cup of your favorite BBQ rub. Then, coat the meat of the chops with Chipotle Adobo Rub Paste. Be careful not to get the paste on the bone of the chop. Refrigerate for 1 hour.

2. Next, take the chops out of the fridge for 15 minutes prior to putting on a hot grill. Place the lamb chops on a searing hot grill for 4 minutes per side. Take the chops off of the grill. Let them rest for 3–5 minutes.

3. Prior to serving at the tailgate, wrap the bone of the chop in a piece of parchment tied with a ribbon or kitchen twine to make for a mess-free eating experience (see picture). Serve with Poblano Lime Dipping Sauce. So. Good!

Chipotle Adobo Rub Paste

4. Add all ingredients to the food processor. Process into a paste.

Poblano Lime Dipping Sauce

5. Slice charred poblano peppers open and scrape their seeds. Roughly chop. Add remaining ingredients. Squeeze the roasted garlic "paste" into the mixture. Place all ingredients in a food processor and process until smooth.

6. Refrigerate for 30 minutes. Serve alongside the Adobo Lamb Pops. Fresh meets smoky has never tasted so good!

Roasted Garlic and Charred Peppers

7. Place the whole head of garlic with the top of the head sliced off (the furry root-about 1/16th of an inch) in an oven/grill-safe dish. Drizzle with olive oil. Roast until browned and soft, about 30 minutes—inner part of the garlic should have a paste like texture. While roasting the garlic, char the poblanos on a live-fire grill or open flame.

ALLY'S SOUTHERN HEAT—SPICY PORK CHOPS

Did you ever meet someone and know immediately you liked them and that they would be a friend for the duration? Well, that's exactly what happened when I met my talented friend Ally Phillips, the famed boho food and lifestyle blogger. Not only is she an exceptional recipe goddess, she's funny, has an awesome accent from "the hollers of West Virginia," and is one of my best pals. We met when we were MasterChef contestants, sequestered together as roomies for weeks. The bonding began the moment I walked into our shared hotel room and saw her smilin' face . . . the rest is history! When I asked her for a recipe, she happily shared a tailgate recipe that embodies her deliciously boho bold style. Enjoy the flavors! Just like the author of this recipe, it is special!

Makes 4–10 servings, depending on how they are served—Ally gives us options!

2 Tbsp. extra virgin olive oil

2 tsp. Tony Chachere's Original Creole Seasoning

2 tsp. dry harissa

½ tsp. sea salt

4 premium thick boneless pork chops, about 1¼-inch to 1½-inch thick

6 kosher dills, dice into ½-inch pieces

3 Tbsp. classic yellow mustard

3 Tbsp. Dijon mustard

4 slices pita bread, soft, cut into triangles

1. Heat a nonstick large skillet on medium-high heat. When hot, reduce to medium heat. Add the olive oil.

2. Put the creole seasoning, harissa, and salt in a pie plate. Blend together. Coat the chops with cooking spray on both sides. Lay the chops in the pie plate and coat each side with the spice mixture. Put in the hot skillet. Cook, covered, on each side 3–4 minutes.

3. Remove pork chops and place on a cutting board. Put foil over the chops and let them rest for 5 minutes. Cut the chops into bite-sized pieces, about 6–8 bites per chop, or serve whole. Use toothpicks to skewer a dill-pickle slice then a pork bite. Serve with mustard for dipping and wedges of soft pita bread.

BACON PIMENTO JALAPEÑO CHEESE SANDWICH ON A PRETZEL BUN

Spicy, cheesy, and savory. Creamy, melty pimento cheese atop a fresh pretzel bun. Served with crisp bacon and sautéed jalapeno slices. This hearty sandwich may be the official sandwich of southern tailgating.

Makes 6–8 servings

2 Tbsp. butter

6 jalapeño peppers, seeded, ribs removed; 2 peppers minced, 2 peppers sliced

6-8 pretzel buns

2½ cup shredded white cheddar cheese

2½ cups of shredded cheddar cheese

1 (4-oz.) jar pimento peppers

¾ cup mayonnaise

1 lb. bacon, cooked crisp and chopped

½ tsp. black pepper

½ tsp. garlic powder

½ tsp. cayenne pepper

1. In a large skillet, melt 1 tablespoon of butter. Sauté the sliced jalapeño in the butter. Remove from pan and set aside. In the same pan, toast the insides of the bottom and top of the pretzel buns. Remove from pan and set aside. Place the remaining 1 tablespoon of butter and the remaining jalapeño peppers in the skillet. Sauté the peppers until translucent. Take off heat and let cool.

2. In a medium mixer bowl with a paddle attachment, combine the cheese, pimentos, minced sautéed peppers, mayonnaise, bacon, black pepper, garlic powder, and cayenne. Mix at a low speed until thoroughly combined. Cover and refrigerate for 2 hours.

3. On a sheet pan, lay out the bottom of the toasted pretzel roll. Spread the pimento mixture on the inside of the pretzel bread. Add the sliced jalapeños to the top of the pimento cheese spread. Next, take the top roll and spread a thin smear of the of the pimento cheese on the inside. Put the two pieces of bread together. Bake until the sandwiches are warm and melty. Enjoy!

BUFFALO CHICKEN PIZZA WITH CARAMELIZED RED ONIONS

The reason that these hand-formed pizzas look like UFOs is that they are out-of-this-world delicious. Pre-bake the crust and prep the ingredients at home. Then pack it all up and finish the assembly and warm-up real quick on the grill. The caramelized onion topping adds a really special touch, so don't skip it. It seems like it might not be worth that extra step, but it's what makes this pizza the best ever.

Makes 16 servings

Buffalo Chicken Pizza with Caramelized Red Onions

⅛ cup unbleached flour for preparing the pans

2 (16-oz.) balls store-bought pizza dough

2 Tbsp. olive oil

Parmesan cheese, to sprinkle on each crust

Buffalo Chicken Topping (recipe below)

2 cups Colby Jack cheese

Caramelized Onions (recipe below)

Frank's Red Hot Sauce, for drizzling

blue cheese crumbles, for topping

Buffalo Chicken Topping

meat from 1 store-bought rotisserie roasted chicken, cold, skin removed, meat finely diced

32 oz. cream cheese, softened

Beth's Wing Sauce (recipe below)

2 cups Colby Jack cheese

1 cup celery, finely diced and sautéed

Beth's Wing Sauce

½ cup butter, melted

1 cup Frank's Red Hot Sauce

2 tsp. of cayenne pepper powder

½ tsp. of brown sugar

Caramelized Onions

3 Tbsp. olive oil

1 Tbsp. butter

2 large red onions, thinly sliced

1 tsp. salt

1 tsp. sugar

Buffalo Chicken Pizza with Caramelized Red Onions

1. Preheat the oven to 500 degrees.

2. Sprinkle a pizza stone, pizza pan, or baking sheet lightly with flour. Press the dough with your fingers until it's as flat as possible. Pull the dough over your fists and gently pull the edges outward while rotating the crust. When the dough is at a 12-inch diameter with a 1½-inch thickness, drizzle with the olive oil, sprinkle with parmesan cheese, then, put it on the floured pan.

3. Bake the dough for 8 minutes. Make sure the crust is rotated frequently to ensure even baking. Remove from oven and cool for 15 minutes.

4. Once cooled, spread Buffalo Chicken Topping over the top of crust. Then, sprinkle one cup of cheese over each pizza. Top with caramelized onions. Bake for another 5–8 minutes to warm the topping and melt the cheese. Drizzle with Frank's Red Hot Sauce. Top with blue cheese crumbles and serve! Yum!

Buffalo Chicken Topping

5. Blend all ingredients together. Set aside until crust is cooled.

Beth's Wing Sauce

6. On medium heat in a medium saucepan, whisk together the ingredients. Bring to a simmer. Turn off heat and let cool.

Caramelized Onions

7. Heat oil in a large sauté pan over low heat. Add butter, red onions, and salt. Cook very slowly for 15–20 minutes, stirring occasionally to prevent them from sticking to the pan. When onions are softened and dark, add the sugar. Slowly stir and cook on low for another 5–10 minutes.

CAPRESE PESTO TRIFLE

Trifles look beautiful on a party table. Not only are they pretty, but they can be assembled quickly with very little cooking if you use ready-made ingredients. To add a fresh twist, I bring salad and dessert together in this savory ode to the trifle. Caprese flavors of cheese, pesto, and tomatoes are a hit with most crowds. I add crunchy, creamy layers to create a true fan favorite. Use a traditional glass-stemmed trifle bowl or an oversized jar with a top to carry and serve this not-so-traditional trifle. Bring a long-handled spoon to get to the bottom of the jar or bowl, because you and your fellow fans will want one of each layer for optimal tailgating pleasure.

Makes 8–12 servings

Caprese Pesto Trifle

1 cup part-skim ricotta

6 Tbsp. pesto

3 Tbsp. grated Parmesan cheese

1 tsp. salt, plus ½ tsp., plus ¼ tsp.

1 tsp. fresh cracked black pepper, plus ½ tsp., plus ¼ tsp.

16 oz. fresh mozzarella

6 Tbsp. balsamic vinegar

2 Tbsp. extra virgin olive oil

2 cups baby arugula

1 Tbsp. lemon juice

2 large tomatoes, finely diced

¼ cup packed basil leaves (about 20–30 leaves)

3 cups croutons, homemade or store-bought (recipe for Ciabatta Croutons below)

2 avocados, peeled, pitted, and diced

Ciabatta Croutons

1 large loaf ciabatta bread

3 Tbsp. olive oil

1 Tbsp. grated Parmesan cheese

2 tsp. garlic salt

1 tsp. dried oregano

Caprese Pesto Trifle

1. Preheat the oven to 350 degrees.

2. In a medium bowl, whisk together the ricotta, pesto, Parmesan, 1 teaspoon of salt, and 1 teaspoon of pepper. In another medium bowl, mix together the mozzarella, vinegar, olive oil, ½ teaspoon of salt, and ½ teaspoon of pepper. In another medium bowl, toss the arugula, lemon juice, ¼ teaspoon of salt, and ¼ teaspoon of pepper.

3. Layer ingredients in a glass serving dish, smoothing a ¼-inch-thick layer of the ricotta mixture at the bottom of the dish. Next, add a layer of the arugula. Top with half of the diced tomato and a layer of basil leaves. Then, layer with half the mozzarella mixture, and then add a layer each of croutons and avocado. Repeat until the last layer, which should be the ricotta pesto.

Ciabatta Croutons

4. Slice the ciabatta loaf into ½-inch cubes and place in a large bowl. Drizzle with olive oil and toss until all the bread is coated. Sprinkle with the cheese, garlic salt, and oregano. Toss to evenly season the bread.

5. Spread the seasoned bread cubes onto a parchment-lined cookie sheet in a single layer. Bake for 20 minutes or until croutons are crisp and golden brown. Let cool.

CORNED BEEF SWISS AND COLESLAW SLIDERS

These are just little gems. Very quick to make and they transport easily. As fast as you set them on the tailgate table is as fast as you can grab your platter back. Consider a double batch, while you're at it.

Makes 12 servings

1 package coleslaw mix (blend of shredded green and red cabbage and carrots)

½ cup store-bought coleslaw salad dressing

¼ cup relish

2 Tbsp. grainy mustard

24 mini dark rye breads

1½ lb. thinly sliced deli corned beef

12 (2-inch) squares of Swiss cheese

2 Tbsp. mayonnaise

1. Preheat the oven to 350 degrees.

2. In a large bowl, combine the coleslaw mix, dressing, 1 Tbsp. of relish, and 1 Tbsp. of mustard, 1 Tbsp. of mayo. Mix well. Refrigerate the slaw for 30 minutes.

3. Place the rye bread squares on a sheet pan. Top each with a dollop of mustard, mayo and relish. Pile two slices of corned beef on each bread square. Cover with a piece of Swiss cheese. Place in the oven for 5–7 minutes to melt the cheese and warm the bread.

4. On a separate sheet pan, toast the remaining rye bread. Once the open-face sandwiches are melty and the bread is toasted, assemble the sandwiches by scooping the slaw mixture onto the cheese and top with a square of toasted bread. Skewer the sandwiches with a pendant-adorned pick and serve these cuties immediately.

EGG AND POTATO BUNDLERS
• BACON •

"Want s'm eggs?" What was that? You may have slurred your words. Oh, I get it . . . some eggs! Yes, I don't mind if I do! I've created these fun and hearty hot bundlers for early-morning tailgates that turn into late nights. Eating one can sustain a serious reveler through a long day of fun. They are hearty, satisfying, and ever so portable.

Attach a fork and napkin to each for the complete turnkey experience. To keep them warm, place the wrapped potatoes in a large soft cooler and set the cooler right on the table. Lift up the top of the cooler when you're ready to serve, and voila! It's bundle time!

Makes 12 Bundlers

12 large baking potatoes, baked
   (oil and salt the potatoes prior to baking)

3 Tbsp. butter, melted

salt and pepper to taste

1 lb. breakfast bacon, cooked and roughly
   chopped

16 oz. Monterey Jack and cheddar blend cheese

12 eggs

1 bunch green onions, thinly sliced

1. Preheat the oven to 450 degrees.

2. Use a sharp paring knife to score an oval in the middle of the baked potato, and cut down into the potato. Gently scoop out the insides with a spoon, leaving a ¼-inch layer of potato. Avoid puncturing the bottom or slicing too deeply into the potato.

3. Brush the interior of the potato with butter and sprinkle with salt and pepper. Layer the potato with bacon and cheese. Individually crack eggs into a small bowl and pour the egg onto the top of each partially filled potato. Repeat until all the baked potatoes are filled.

4. Place the filled potatoes on a baking sheet. Bake for 5 minutes or until the eggs are solid. Once the eggs are solid, sprinkle sliced green onions over each potato. Wrap each potato in a 6" × 6" piece of foil. Once the eggs are solid, wrap each potato in a 6" × 6" piece of foil. Tie a disposable fork (I like the cute wooden forks purchased on Etsy.com, Amazon.com, or at Target) and a napkin to each bundle with kitchen twine. Serve with a dollop of sour cream, if desired. Warm up your friends at early-morning tailgates and they will give you a hearty high-five!

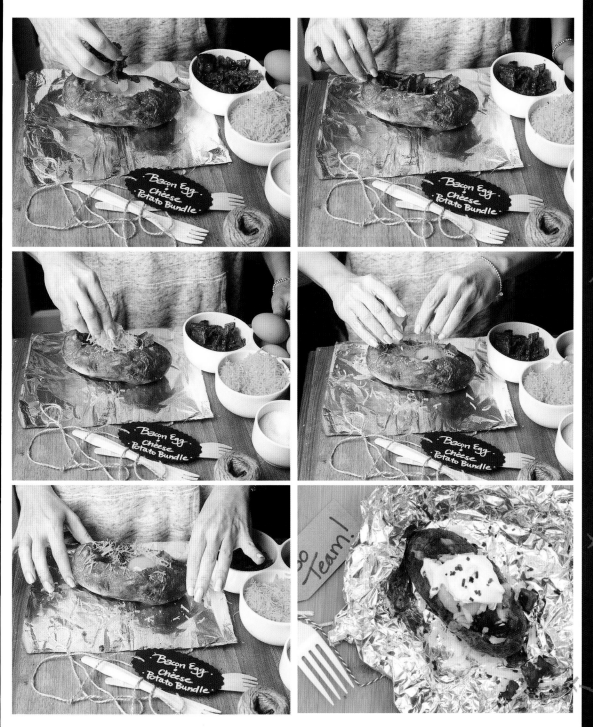

EGG AND POTATO BUNDLERS
• CHORIZO •

Makes 12 Bundlers

12 large baking potatoes, baked
(oil and salt the potatoes prior to baking)

1 lb. Mexican chorizo, browned

1 (16-oz.) jar salsa

2 cups shredded cheddar cheese

12 eggs

8 oz. sour cream (optional)

1. Preheat the oven to 450 degrees.

2. Use a sharp paring knife to score an oval in the middle of the baked potato, and cut down into the potato. Gently scoop out the insides with a spoon, leaving a ¼-inch layer of potato. Avoid puncturing the bottom or slicing too deeply into the potato.

3. Mix the browned chorizo, salsa, and ¾ cup of shredded cheese in a large bowl. Fill each potato about three-fourths full. Individually crack each egg into a small bowl, and pour each egg onto the top of each partially filled potato. Repeat until all the baked potatoes are filled.

4. Place the filled potatoes on a baking sheet. Bake for 5 minutes or until the eggs are solid. Once the eggs are solid, wrap each potato in a 6" × 6" piece of foil. Tie a disposable fork (I like the cute wooden forks purchased on Etsy.com, Amazon. com, or at Target) and a napkin to each bundle with kitchen twine. Serve with a dollop of sour cream, if desired. Warm up your friends at early-morning tailgates and they will give you a hearty high-five!

EGG AND POTATO BUNDLERS
• MAPLE SAUSAGE •

Makes 12 Bundlers

12 large baking potatoes, baked
(oil and salt the potatoes prior to baking)

1 lb. breakfast sausage, cooked and diced

8 oz. high-quality maple syrup

2 cups queso fresco cheese
(I know—it seems like it won't go, but trust me.)

12 eggs

1. Preheat the oven to 450 degrees.

2. Use a sharp paring knife to score an oval in the middle of the baked potato, and cut down into the potato. Gently scoop out the insides with a spoon, leaving a ¼-inch layer of potato. Avoid puncturing the bottom or slicing too deeply into the potato.

3. Layer each potato with the browned sausage, syrup (about 2 tablespoons of syrup per potato), and ¼ cup of queso fresco cheese. Individually crack each egg into a small bowl, and pour each egg onto the top of each partially filled potato. Repeat until all the baked potatoes are filled.

4. Place the filled potatoes on a baking sheet. Bake for 5 minutes or until the eggs are solid. Once the eggs are solid, wrap each potato in a 6" × 6" piece of foil. Tie a disposable fork (I like the cute wooden forks purchased on Etsy.com, Amazon.com, or at Target) and a napkin to each bundle with kitchen twine. Serve with a dollop of sour cream, if desired. Warm up your friends at early-morning tailgates and they will give you a hearty high-five!

JAY'S BLACKBERRY
BONE-IN BOSTON BUTT

This recipe was shared with me by my friend Jay Ducote. Jay is a big deal in southern food, and as an LSU fan, tailgating is one of his superpowers. He is a food and beverage writer, blogger, radio host, culinary personality, and chef from Louisiana. And, get this: He finished runner-up on Season 11 of Food Network Star. *After* Food Network Star, *he had a show called* Deep Fried America *on the Travel Channel. Jay also produces and hosts an award winning show called* The Bite and Booze Radio Show. *As you might imagine, he has a great personality. He has his own Jay D's product line, featuring his Louisiana Barbecue Sauce, Louisiana Molasses Mustard, Spicy & Sweet Barbecue Rub, Jay D's Blanc du Bois, a collaboration with West Monroe's Landry Vineyards, and a coffee line. Needless to say, this award-winning culinary guy knows his way around a grill and a tailgate. I was lucky enough to tailgate at LSU with Jay a couple years ago and got to see his skills firsthand. Such a big day for my taste buds in Baton Rouge. I think that was the day I fell in love with southern tailgating. LSU is a spectacle of all things tailgate on game day. LSU is, definitely, a bucket-list stop if you are a tailgate enthusiast.*

Makes enough to feed a crowd

1 (8-oz.) jar blackberry jam

1 lb. local honey

1 cup apple cider

1 Tbsp. freshly ground black pepper

1 large bone-in pork shoulder (Boston Butt)

1 cup brown sugar

1 cup Slap Ya Mama Cajun Seasoning

Louisiana pecan wood

1. So let's start with the injection. The idea is that we're going to flavor the pork both inside and outside the meat. The ingredients that get injected inside the pork will marinate the meat, as well as provide some bold flavor. Mix the blackberry jam, honey, apple cider, and black pepper together really well. I use a food processor or blender for this part. Once it is all combined, strain the seeds out, if there were seeds in your blackberry jam.

2. Now is the fun part. Lay the trimmed pork shoulder down on a sheet pan and start injecting the blackberry mixture into it. Feel free to take a little sip of the concoction; it should be sweet, fruity, peppery, and have a little kick from the apple cider! Stick your injection needle into the pork shoulder all over the place. Flip the pork over and make sure to get the other side too.

3. Once you have thoroughly injected the mixture into the pork, the next step is to rub the outside. The rub is a simple combination of brown sugar and Slap Ya Mama Cajun Seasoning. That will provide the sweetness of sugar with the saltiness and spiciness of the Slap Ya Mama Cajun Seasoning. The brown sugar will caramelize on the outside

and provide a nice bark, while the salt and peppers will penetrate into the pork and leave it flavorful. Just blend the ingredients together and rub it all over the outside of the pork shoulder. It will mix with the runoff blackberry mixture, but that's okay. Just let it form a paste on the outside of the pork shoulder.

4. Now get your smoker going. As a general rule of thumb, you'll want to smoke the pork shoulder at 200–250 degrees until the internal temperature has maintained around 165–170 degrees. I usually smoke it closer to 200 degrees, so it takes 8–10 hours. The finished product should have a bark on the outside, nice and caramelized. The inside will be tender and juicy.

5. Once you've removed the pork shoulder from your smoker and given it a little time to rest and cool, you should be ready to start pulling it apart. Just grab a handful and go to town! If it won't pull apart with your hands, then it really isn't cooked enough. I hope this recipe brings you as much happiness as it did for me. Enjoy, JD

LAMAR MOORE'S KFC— KOREAN FRIED CHICKEN

Stop what you are doing right now. Look at this masterful recipe created by a master of his craft. Not kidding. This recipe is very special and we are all lucky to have it. Make this for your tailgate, but beware, once people have had it, you are in it for a lifetime. People, being people with taste buds, will like it and want it often. Proceed with caution.

Who is the architect of this recipe that holds such beautiful flavor? The wonderful Chef Lamar Moore is the man! He is a friend and a classically trained and well-traveled chef. Included in his impressive experiences is being a respected pitmaster. Needless to say, this guy knows flavors. All of it, coming at you! The flavors, the crunch, the juicy deliciousness. It's all yours for the taking. Thank you, Chef Lamar!

Makes 8 servings

Pre-Coating

½ cup cornstarch

3 tsp. sea salt

1 Tbsp. baking powder

8 (5-oz.) bone-in airline chicken breasts

peanut oil, for frying

Batter

½ cup cornstarch

1 cup flour

4 Tbsp. Korean chili

1 Tbsp. sea salt

3 Tbsp. garlic powder

3 Tbsp. onion powder

2 Tbsp. baking powder

2 Tbsp. Spanish paprika

½ cup water

½ cup club soda

3 Tbsp. Korean chili paste (*gochujang*)

Korean BBQ Sauce

5 Tbsp. Korean chili paste (*gochujang*)

4 Tbsp. ketchup

2 Tbsp. brown sugar

⅓ cup molasses

2 Tbsp. soy sauce

2 Tbsp. sesame oil

3 Tbsp. ginger, finely chopped

2 Tbsp. garlic, finely choppped

Pre-Coating

1. In a large bowl, whisk together the first 3 ingredients. Add the chicken and toss well. Put in cooler for at least 3 hours.

2. Add the peanut oil to a heavy-duty pot. Heat to 350 degrees.

Batter

3. In a large bowl, whisk together the dry ingredients. In a smaller bowl, whisk together the wet ingredients. Right before you fry, whisk the wet mixture into the dry mixture.

4. Dip each piece of chicken into the batter. Fry the chicken until G.B.D. (Golden Brown and Delicious), 12–15 minutes or until the internal temperature is between 160 and 165 degrees. Transfer fried chicken to a wire rack to drain.

Korean BBQ Sauce

5. Combine all ingredients in a pot. Mix until well incorporated. Dip fried chicken in sauce. Serve immediately.

E3VIP FIRE SHRIMP

My friend Richard Carrier shared this killer recipe, and although it is a seafood recipe, it is as Midwestern as they come. Richard is a well-known luxury tailgate pioneer. He is the founder of E3VIP, one of the first luxury tailgate companies in the US and named by Bon Appétit as the Best Tailgate Experience in America. He created this delicious recipe that has been served at many, many Chicago Bears games in the parking lot of Soldier Field. That makes this tasty recipe an important part of our midwestern tailgate culture! Please enjoy some exceptional seafood from the prairie!

Makes 15 servings

¼ cup extra virgin olive oil

½ stick Kerry Gold salted butter, melted

2 oz. Cholula sauce

cracked Himalayan salt to taste

fresh cracked pepper to taste

crushed red pepper to taste

1 lb. (15 count) jumbo shrimp, deveined, shell on

lemons, for finishing

On the day before your event:

1. Whisk ingredients from olive oil through crushed red pepper together in a medium bowl. Add thawed shrimp and mix. Store in Ziploc bags or appropriate container.

Grill

2. For best results, use a smoking hot charcoal grill—Gas will do, too! Grill shrimp for 4–5 minutes on each side. Finish with a squeeze of fresh lemon juice. Place immediately on a warm tray with cocktail napkins.

MOMMA'S POTATO SALAD

This potato salad has a secret. It's a little different than the rest. This is my mom's recipe, and for years, my sister and I could not figure out what made it so darn good. We knew that the olives were a special touch . . . but what else did she do to make it have that distinctly unique and "make 'em come back for more" flavor? What would any Italian momma do when spicing up an American tradition? Add a little garlicky Italian salad dressing and olives and . . . Oh, momma mia, it's delizioso!

Makes 20 servings

5 lbs. potatoes

10 eggs, hardboiled, peeled; 8 diced, 2 sliced and reserved for garnish

½ cup Italian salad dressing (make your own or use a store-bought brand)

1 small onion, chopped

3 green onions, chopped

3 stalks celery, chopped

1 jar Spanish olives, finely chopped

1 cup mayonnaise

1 tsp. celery salt

pepper to taste

¼ celery leaves, chopped

1. Peel the potatoes and chop them into small cubes. Place them in a large pot of salted water. Boil potatoes over medium heat until tender, 12–14 minutes. Drain the potatoes. Refrigerate to cool.

2. Place the 8 diced hardboiled eggs in a large decorative bowl.

3. Stir in Italian dressing, onion, green onions, celery, olives, and mayonnaise with the eggs, then add celery salt and pepper to taste. Let the mixture chill in the refrigerator at least 30 minutes to incorporate the flavors.

4. Mix in the chilled chopped potatoes. Refrigerate for at least another 30 minutes.

5. For garnish, lay the reserved, sliced hardboiled eggs along the top of the salad. Sprinkle the salad with a bit of paprika and a sprig of celery leaf for garnish. Serve cold.

SWEET HEAT PULLED PORK AND UDON NOODLES

There's nothing like holding and slurping up a warm cup of noodles on cold game-day afternoon. Making a homemade noodle dish seems like so much work though, doesn't it? I've eliminated some of the prep by giving you some pre-cooked elements to use in this dish. Start with pre-seasoned pulled pork—my favorite is ROWDYDOW bbQ. You make the base broth, add the finishing touches, and just like that, you have comfort food that's hot, ready, and loved by your tailgate crew! Oh, yes . . . There's a slow-cooker involved, so it's part of the three-easy club: easy making, easy transporting, and easy serving. Now that's easy!

Makes enough to feed a crowd

Sweet Heat Pulled Pork and Udon Noodles

2 Tbsp. vegetable oil

1½ lb. mix of shiitake and oyster mushrooms, thinly sliced

2 shallots, thinly sliced

6 scallions, thinly sliced diagonally

3 Tbsp. fresh ginger, thinly sliced

2 garlic cloves, minced

2 jalapeño peppers, seeded and thinly sliced

64 oz. mushroom stock

½ lb. spinach, de-stemmed, roughly chopped

1 small bunch Thai basil, chiffonade; reserve some whole leaves for garnish

2 Tbsp. Sriracha, reserve some for garnish

2 Tbsp. soy sauce

juice of 1 lime, plus wedges of lime for garnish

1 tsp. sesame oil

2 lb. ROWDYDOW bbQ Pulled Pork in Sweet Vinegar BBQ Sauce (buy online)

salt to taste

32 oz. Caramelized Japanese Udon Noodles (instructions below)

Caramelized Japanese Udon Noodles

32 oz. precooked packaged Japanese Udon Noodles

a pinch of salt

2 Tbsp. sesame oil, plus some for drizzling

Sweet Heat Pulled Pork and Udon Noodles

1. Heat the oil in a sauté pan. Sauté the next 6 ingredients, from mushrooms through jalapeno

2. In a crockpot on high heat, add the mushroom broth, spinach, Thai basil, Sriracha, and the sauteed ingredients. Let cook for two hours. After two hours, turn crockpot heat down to low and add soy sauce, lime juice, and sesame oil. Let cook for 30 minutes. Break apart the pulled pork to shred into the broth. Add salt to taste.

3. Add Caramelized Japanese Udon Noodles right before serving. Garnish individual bowls of this yummy goodness with a lime wedge, a drizzle of Sriracha, and a drizzle of sesame oil. Don't stop there—make it pretty and fragrant by topping this masterpiece with two lovely Thai basil leaves. Oh baby, this is sooooo good! #GoTeamSweetHeat!

Caramelized Japanese Udon Noodles

4. Remove the noodles from the package. Pat dry with a paper towel, and sprinkle with salt. In a large sauté pan on high heat, add the sesame oil. As soon as you see the ripple of the oil, add the noodles. Quickly sauté and brown the noodles until they are browned and have an almost-crispy texture. Set aside.

KERRY'S BIG BITE PASTRAMI WITH PANCETTA GIARDINIERA AND ARTICHOKE SPREAD

My sister, Kerry, is one of the most amazing super-sandwich makers around. This hearty, man-sized sandwich is her masterpiece. It's built on layers and layers of toasted melty cheese, piled high with stacks of pastrami—but that's not all. She brilliantly adds a twist of not just one flavor-enhancing creamy spread, but amps it to the stratosphere with a flavor layer of crispy Pancetta Giardiniera! What's giardiniera, you ask? If you don't know, make this sandwich and your taste buds will thank you! There are a few steps to make this sandwich, but I promise it's worth it! One of the best you'll ever eat, a serious crowd pleaser. So make this ahead for game day by wrapping it all up in tinfoil after it's been built, and place it in a cooler that you've designated for warm food.

Makes 4–6 servings

Kerry's Big Bite Pastrami with Pancetta Giardiniera and Artichoke Spread

4-6 ciabatta rolls, halved

1½ cups Jalapeño Artichoke Spread (recipe below)

1 lb. Swiss cheese

1½ lbs. thinly sliced premium pastrami

Pancetta Giardiniera (recipe below)

1 cup jarred marinated artichokes

Jalapeno Artichoke Spread

1 (8-oz.) package cream cheese, softened

4 oz. grated Parmesan cheese

6 oz. finely grated mozzarella cheese

1 Tbsp. mayonnaise

1 (6 oz.) jar marinated artichokes, finely chopped

1 (6 oz.) jar pickled jalapeno, diced

1 tsp. garlic salt

Pancetta Giardiniera

8 oz. pancetta, finely diced

1 (16-oz.) jar of your favorite jarred giardiniera, oil drained

Kerry's Big Bite Pastrami with Pancetta Giardiniera and Artichoke Spread

1. Make the Pancetta Giardiniera and the Jalapeño Artichoke Spread.

2. Preheat the oven to 425 degrees.

3. Toast the halved ciabatta rolls by placing them inside down on a warm skillet that still has the rendered fat from crisping the pancetta. Once the rolls are toasted, smear a thick layer of the Jalapeño Artichoke Spread on the inside of the bottom half of the roll. Add cheese, pastrami, a small dollop of more spread, and a generous scoop of Pancetta Giardiniera. Add another layer of pastrami and cheese again. Next, add a marinated artichoke and one more layer of cheese.

4. Bake in the oven with the top of the roll off of the sandwich, cheese exposed, until the cheese is melted.

Jalapeno Artichoke Spread

5. In a medium bowl, combine all of the ingredients. Mix until well incorporated. Refrigerate for 10 minutes prior to spreading on sandwich.

Pancetta Giardiniera

6. In a small skillet, brown the diced pancetta until crisp and caramelized. Turn off the heat and add the giardiniera. Place the mixture in a small bowl and set aside.

7. Tip: Reserve the oils used to caramelize the pancetta in the skillet. You will toast the ciabatta roll using the rendered fat from the pancetta.

CHAPTER 6
THE EXTRA POINT

DIY Tailgate Party

Do you want to be all extra? You may say no, but everyone secretly wants to be extra. Here's your chance to ramp up everything you've ever known to be a typical tailgate to something truly extra. This is where your supermodels of tailgate decor and buffets live. Get the hashtags ready and cameras perched because this is Instagram territory, people. #tailgateceleb #instafamous!

BETH'S CHILI WITH MUSHROOMS & BLACK BEANS

Vegans and vegetarians or anyone that just wants a delicious chili, here is your bold and delicious option! Enjoy with all the same accoutrements! I have also included a Lime Cashew Crema, for your cool and bright element without the dairy. I'm good to you like that.

Makes 15 servings

Beth's Chili with Mushrooms & Black Beans

2 Tbsp. olive oil

1 yellow onion, diced

1 red bell pepper, diced

2 carrots, peeled and diced

½ tsp. sea salt

1 lb. button mushrooms, quartered

1 lb. Portobello mushrooms, sliced and halved

2 tsp. red pepper flakes

2 garlic cloves, minced

36 oz. chopped tomatoes

36 oz. black beans, drained

2 Tbsp. miso pasta or soy sauce

2 cups vegetable stock

3 Tbsp. ground cumin

1½ Tbsp. smoked paprika

2 tsp. dried oregano

Garnish

Lime and Cilantro Cashew Crema

salsa

brown rice

lime wedges

Lime and Cilantro Cashew Crema

1 cup whole raw cashews, soaked overnight in water with a pinch of salt

½ cup water

½ bunch fresh cilantro

3 garlic cloves, roasted and squeezed into a paste

zest and juice of 2 limes

1½ tsp. apple cider vinegar

½ tsp. kosher salt

½ tsp. white pepper

Beth's Chili with Mushrooms & Black Beans

1. In a large skillet on medium-low heat, add the oil, onion, bell pepper, carrots, and salt. Sauté until the onions are translucent and the carrots are softened.

2. Bring the heat to medium-high and add the mushrooms to the skillet. Cook until the mushrooms are softened. Next, add the red pepper flakes and garlic. Once incorporated, add the tomatoes and beans.

3. In a medium bowl, whisk together the miso and vegetable stock until combined. Add this mixture to the skillet. Bring to a simmer. Cover and cook over the lowest heat for an hour. Taste and adjust your seasonings as needed. *Or* place all ingredients in a slow cooker for 3 hours. Garnish with Lime and Cilantro Cashew Crema, salsa, brown rice, and lime wedges. Serve.

Lime and Cilantro Cashew Crema

4. Place all of the ingredients in a food processor. Process until smooth. Refrigerate for 1 hour prior to serving with the chili.

GAME-DAY CHILI

This is the chili that if you have not other chili on your Chili Bar, you would absolutely need to have. It's the beefy, spicy, chunky chili that people love. It's a belly-warmer, and it's fun to dress up with all sorts of crunchy, crispy, cool, fresh ingredients.

Makes 15–20 servings

3 lbs. 80/20 ground beef, cooked and drained

2 yellow onions, chopped

2 Tbsp olive oil

2 yellow bell peppers, cored, seeded, and chopped

2 red bell peppers, cored, seeded, and chopped 2 (4 oz.) cans green chilies

2 tsp. chili powder

4 tsp. ground cumin

1 tsp. dried red pepper flakes

½ tsp. cayenne pepper, or to taste

2 tsp. salt

3 (32-oz.) cans diced tomatoes

2 (16-oz.) cans of your favorite red kidney beans, drained and rinsed

2 (16-oz.) cans of your favorite black beans drained and rinsed black pepper to taste

1. In a Dutch oven, brown the meat until it's cooked thoroughly. Drain the meat and set it aside.

2. In a pan over medium-low heat, cook the onions in oil until translucent. Add the bell peppers, green chilies, chili powder, cumin, red pepper flakes, cayenne, black pepper and salt. Cook for 5 minutes.

3. Add tomatoes (with juice), beans, and browned meat. Bring to a boil. Let boil for 5 minutes. Reduce heat and simmer, uncovered, for 45 minutes, stirring occasionally.

OR

4. Place all of the ingredients in a slow cooker for 3 hours on high. Reduce heat to medium and cook for 3 more hours. Serve with accoutrements. If you notice a layer of grease on top of the chili as it settles, make sure to scoop the extra grease off the top of the chili before serving.

ITALIAN CHILI MAC

It's pasta—no, it's chili . . . wait. It's a tailgate fusion! Beans, pasta, cumin, mozzarella, and San Marzano tomatoes. It feels confused but at the same time amazing. It's comfort food no matter which way you look at it. A hearty tummy-filler that you can set and forget. Just remember to reserve the noodles for right before serving.

Makes 10 servings

2 Tbsp. olive oil

1½ lbs. ground beef

2 Tbsp. chili powder

1 tsp. salt

1 tsp. pepper

1 small yellow onion, diced

1 red bell pepper, seeded and chopped

8 oz. baby bella mushrooms, stemmed and sliced

4 garlic cloves, chopped

1 cup beef stock

1 can San Marzano tomatoes, crushed

4–5 basil leaves, roughly chopped

16 oz. canned red kidney beans

1 Tbsp. cumin

½ bottle Heinz 57 Sauce

1 lb. macaroni noodles, cooked and set aside until ready to serve

16 oz. shredded mozzarella

store-bought garlic bread, sliced

1. In a large pan, warm the olive oil. Add the beef, chili powder, salt and pepper. Cook the meat until browned.

2. Add the onions, peppers, mushrooms, and garlic. Cook for 6–7 minutes. Add the stock, red kidney beans, cumin, Heinz 57 Sauce and the tomatoes. Let the sauce simmer for 10 minutes, and then add the basil at the last minute.

3. Put the cooked noodles in a casserole dish. Add the meat sauce. Sprinkle with shredded mozzarella and serve with slices of garlic bread.

WHITE CHICKEN CHILI MAC BREAD BOWLS

This main dish does double duty as a belly-filler and hand-warmer, all at the same time. The best part about this flavor-filled, hefty dish? Everyone gets his or her own toasty bread bowl full of goodness. Believe me, people will ask for this recipe over and over. It's a legend, for sure.

Wrap the pre-cut rolls in foil and warm them before leaving home. At the tailgate, ladle the chili into the bread bowls. The chili should stay warm in the slow cooker for 2–3 hours. If you have the option to plug in the slow cooker, keep the chili on warm. If you'd like, serve the bread bowls with condiments, such as bowls of shredded cheese, sour cream, chopped cilantro, wedges of lime, and oyster crackers.

Makes 12 servings

1 medium onion, finely diced

4 chicken breasts (about 2 lbs. total)

2 large jalapeño peppers, roasted and seeded

48 oz. chicken broth

2 (8-oz.) cans green chilies, drained

juice of 2 limes, reserve half

1 Tbsp. salt, plus ½ Tbsp. reserved

1 Tbsp. olive oil

1 tsp. cumin powder, plus ½ tsp. reserved

1 tsp. white pepper, plus ½ tsp. reserved

1 tsp. chili powder, plus ½ tsp. reserved

2 (16-oz.) cans white beans, drained

¾ cup cilantro, roughly chopped, reserve some for garnish

1 (16-oz.) bag frozen white corn

32 oz. grated Mexican cheese blend

½ cup sour cream

1 (16-oz.) bag small elbow or ditalini pasta, boiled to al dente (9-12 min)

12 large sourdough rolls or pretzel rolls (about 4 inches in diameter), with the top cut and center bread scooped out

1. Place all ingredients from onion to chili powder in a slow cooker. Cook for 2½–3 hours on high. Check the chicken to see if it is ready for shredding. At this point, the chicken should be falling apart. Place the chicken on a cutting board. Shred the chicken using two forks.

2. Fold the shredded chicken back into the slow cooker. Add white beans, cilantro, corn, the remaining lime juice and the reserved ½ teaspoon of cumin, white pepper and chili powder. Cook on low for 30 minutes. Turn off heat.

3. Add the cheese blend and melt it into the chili, stirring to coat the chicken. Gently stir in the sour cream, reserved cilantro, and reserved ½ tablespoon of salt. Add the cooked pasta to the chili immediately before serving to eliminate pasta sog factor. Spoon into sourdough or pretzel bread bowls and serve.

CHILI BAR

As the weather cools down and football games heat up, we turn to our slow cookers to help us make all that is warm and comforting. Chili for the win! It's extremely easy to customize, and it's hard to find someone who doesn't enjoy big bowl of one of the varieties that I have shared in this section. Here's a great play on this fan favorite. Pull together a DIY Chili Bar at your next tailgating party, complete with multiple stews, creamy toppings, and crunchy bits to sprinkle atop big hearty bowls full. If you are making a chili bar for a smaller crowd or going to a location that doesn't have enough space or allow for slow cookers, a fun way to bring chili is in a large thermos. Easy to transport and serve from too.

The Chili Bar is a go-to buffet that will make all the tailgaters say, "Hip, hip, hooray!" Pulling a Game-Day Chili Bar together takes a few recipes of slow-cooking chili and some fab accoutrements. You'll need to prepare 3–5 different types of chili or soup, depending on the size of your crowd, and with the recipes in this chapter, you are good to go! Display a spread of awesome toppings and breads for scooping up every chunky bite. These tips can help you make the most of your Game-Day Chili Bar party.

Ideas for Game-Day Chili Accoutrements

Variety. Depending on the crowd, you'll need to prepare 3–5 different types of chili or soup. See the list I have shared here. From Vegetarian Chili to White Chicken Chili to a Chunky Beefy Game-Day Chili, you'll have your team covered.

Cool. Cheese, sour cream and crema are the perfect add-in to chili because they cool the heat of the spices and the temperature of the chili. No doubt chili can stand on its own—these lovely dollops and sprinkles are an extra not to be missed to balance flavors in just the coolest way.

- cojita cheese
- queso fresco
- cheddar cheese
- Monterey Jack cheese
- Chihuahua cheese
- sour cream
- avocado
- avocado crema

Crunch. Crunchy and crispy are the two most important words that help sell snacks, because our brains love crunchy, crispy things. I would go into the science here, but it gets a little thick. Trust me when I tell you that crunchy and crispy are really good things when it comes to adding that extra something special atop chili. Here are toppings full of crunch and crisp for your scientifically satisfying Game-Day Chili Bar!

- tortilla chips
- oyster crackers
- Fritos
- tater tots
- popcorn

Fresh. Bring up that fresh and bright. Deep and intense spicy and beefy chili needs an opposite to lift all of the flavors. Consider adding a bit of fresh to really complete the flavor profile of chili.

- lime wedges
- cilantro, chopped
- jalapenos, minced and seeded
- green onions, minced
- red onions, minced
- pickled onions

Extras. Roasted Poblano Cheddar Cornbread in a Cast-Iron Skillet (see recipe on page 141)

hot sauce—a variety is fun!

crazy-hot peppers—ghost, cayenne, habanero . . . Put a warning on these, though. Most folks can't handle the heat.

How to Build Your Bar. Use slow cookers to cook your variety of chili. Bring them to the tailgate table and line them along the midline of the table. In linen-lined baskets, add your variety of add-ins and toppings. For each type of chili, I like to have separate accoutrements because sometimes the different chilis require different accoutrements. It's a little more work, but it looks better and functions better, too.

Bring big baskets of tortilla chips and small bowls of the variety of accoutrements placed inside large flat-bottom short-walled baskets. I use oval or square baskets for this. They are sturdy with handles and act as serving trays for the accoutrements.

Don't forget to bring disposable (not plastic, if you can help it) spoons, forks, small serving utensils/tongs for each of the accoutrements, ladles for the chili, and . . . napkins!

Bring serving bowls for the chili. Look for disposable high-walled bowls to serve the chili in. They have them at party stores or online. I specifically call these out because they are perfect for tailgating. The wider, shorter-walled bowls are messy at a tailgate. Messy is no fun!

POPPIN' POPCORN RECIPES

I remember making popcorn with my grandfather. My job was to listen for the popping. As soon as the popping started, that's when he would start moving the pot back and forth, fast! He told me that there was magic in popping popcorn. It really did seem like magic because one minute there were just these little yellow kernels, and the next, fluffy white treats. It's one of the most exciting moments in any cooking. Grab a scoop and get poppin'!

You can use microwave popcorn, but I say use fresh-popped popcorn because it's easy to do, less expensive, and it lets you start with a clean slate with no salt or seasonings—plus it's just better tasting. Use an air popper or a large pot on the stove top.

BUFFALO POPCORN

Makes 15–20 servings

¾ cup Buffalo wing sauce

1 cup melted butter

12 cups hot popcorn

1 tsp. garlic powder

1 tsp. celery salt

salt to taste

1. In a small bowl, mix the wing sauce and butter. In a large pot, add popcorn. Add all of the remaining ingredients. Make sure to coat all of the popcorn. Enjoy!

POPCORN ON THE STOVE

Makes 15–20 servings

2 Tbsp. vegetable oil

½ cup popcorn kernels

6-8 quart pot with lid

1. On medium heat, add the oil to the large pot. Warm the oil for 2–3 minutes. Add the kernels. Shake the pan slightly to make sure all of the kernels are covered with oil. Cover with the lid.

2. Listen for popping—once you hear the popcorn start popping, begin to move the pot back and forth on the stove to keep the popcorn from burning. This is very important to keep it movin'. Once the popping stops, remove from heat immediately.

POPPIN' POPCORN RECIPES
CONTINUED

MARSHMALLOW-Y POPCORN (BASE RECIPE)

Makes 15–20 servings

2 cups popcorn

1 (16-oz.) bag of mini marshmallows, melted

4 Tbsp. butter, melted

salt to taste

Add-ins *

chocolate chunks

toffee pieces

mixed nuts

dried fruit

sweet cereal

pretzels

assorted candy pieces (Reese's Pieces, Skittles, Mike n' Ike's, etc.)

* These are simply suggestions; use whatever speaks to your taste buds. Make sure to add at least 3 add-ins, at ¼ cup (for each add-in), to really make your Marshmallow-y Popcorn pop!

1. Spread the popped popcorn on a baking tray lined with parchment paper. In a microwave-safe bowl, melt a bag of marshmallows in the microwave (about 1½ minutes). Add butter, salt, and add-ins to the melted marshmallows.

2. Pour the melty marshmallow mixture over your popcorn mix. Stir together. Let the mixture rest until the marshmallow cools and firms, about 10–15 minutes. Serve in individual cute wax-paper or cellophane bags, or in a large bowl with a scoop.

CARAMELSLOW-COOKERPOPCORN

Makes 15–20 servings

6-quart slow cooker

cooking spray

½ cup butter

1 cup light brown sugar

¼ cup light corn syrup

1 tsp. baking soda

1 tsp. vanilla

12 cups popped popcorn (plain)

2 cups mini pretzel twists

1 cup mixed nuts

1. Coat slow cooker with cooking spray. Add the butter, brown sugar, and corn syrup to the slow cooker. Cover and cook on high for 30 minutes. Rotate the inner bowl of the slow cooker. Continue to cook on high another 30 minutes or until the caramel mixture is bubbling.

2. Remove lid and turn to low. Stir in baking soda and vanilla. Add popcorn and stir well to coat. Continue to cook, uncovered, on low for 1–1½ hours, stirring every 15 to 20 minutes, until popcorn looks like the caramel has dried on it. Spread on waxed paper. Stir in pretzel and nuts.

POPPIN' POPCORN RECIPES
CONTINUED

PARMESAN ROSEMARY POPCORN

Makes 15–20 servings

⅛ tsp. rosemary, very finely minced

1 clove garlic, very finely minced

6 cups popped popcorn

2 tsp. coconut oil

⅓ cup grated Parmesan cheese

salt to taste

pepper to taste

1. Preheat the oven to 300 degrees.

2. Place rosemary on a baking sheet. Bake for 10 minutes or until crisp. Finely process the rosemary and garlic. Set aside.

3. In a small bowl, add coconut oil and rosemary and garlic. Place popcorn in a large bowl and drizzle with coconut oil mixture. Sprinkle with cheese, salt, and pepper. Toss to coat. This is one of my all-time favorites.

ROASTED POBLANO AND CHEDDAR CORNBREAD IN A CAST-IRON SKILLET

This is an excellent addition to the Game-Day Chili Bar. Transport the cornbread in the skillet and serve it directly from it, too. It's a great presentation and, although a bit heavy, it travels nicely (won't break!) Ha! I serve this with the best butter I can find and some local honey. It's a great bite! YUM!

Makes 10 servings

1 (8.5 oz) package cornbread mix

2 Tbsp. olive oil

½ cup fresh or frozen corn

2 cups cheddar cheese, cut into chunks

2 large poblano peppers, roasted (instructions below)

1. Preheat the oven to 450 degrees.

2. Pour oil into a cast-iron skillet and heat in the oven until hot, about 3 minutes.

3. In a large bowl, make the cornbread mixture following the instructions on the box. Fold the corn, cheese, and poblano peppers into the cornbread batter.

4. Remove the skillet from the oven. Pour the batter directly into the pan. It should sizzle a bit.

5. Bake until the crust is golden brown, 25–30 minutes.

Roasted Poblano Peppers

6. Roast the whole poblano peppers directly under a broiler until the skin is charred, turning to char all sides. Remove the skin and seeds. Chop the poblano peppers and set aside.

BETH'S GRILLED APPLE CIDER DONUTS WITH A MAPLE GLAZE

Make these donuts ahead of time, bring them to your tailgate party, dip them in the glaze, and throw them on the grill to warm them up and impress the crowd with homemade GRILLED donuts! There are chunks of warm cinnamon apples filling the donuts with bright sweetness laced throughout. These are a happy treat on a cool fall tailgate morning. Belly-warmer action! Yum!

Makes 12 servings (12 donuts)

Beth's Grilled Apple Cider Donuts with a Maple Glaze

⅓ cup vegetable oil

3 eggs

1¼ cups of brown sugar

1 cup Homemade Chunky Applesauce (recipe below)

¼ cup apple cider

1½ tsp. vanilla extract

1 tsp. ground cinnamon

Pinch of salt

1½ tsp. baking powder

2 cups unbleached flour

Maple Glaze

1½ cups confectioners' sugar

3 Tbsp. maple syrup

2 Tbsp. water

Homemade Chunky Applesauce

1 Tbsp. butter

4 fresh apples, peeled, cored, and chopped into small chunks

1 Tbsp. brown sugar

¾ cup water

1 tsp. freshly squeezed lemon juice

1 tsp. ground cinnamon

¼ tsp. nutmeg

Beth's Grilled Apple Cider Donuts with a Maple Glaze

1. Preheat the oven to 350 degrees.

2. Lightly grease two doughnut pans. Stir together the oil, eggs, sugar, Homemade Chunky Applesauce, cider, vanilla, cinnamon, salt, and baking powder until smooth. Stir in flour until incorporated.

3. Fill each segment of the doughnut pans with ¼ cup of batter, almost to the rim of each segment. Bake for 16–18 minutes. Remove the doughnuts from the oven. Let them cool for a few minutes, and then transfer them to a rack. While the doughnuts are still warm, lay each one, front and back, on a plate full of cinnamon-sugar mix

4. Dip the entire doughnut, front and back, in the Maple Glaze—and here's where it gets fun: Lay the donut on a hot grill. Work it! Get those grill marks on both sides to warm the entire donut. Serve immediately. These are messy and so delicious! Serve with a napkin and in a parchment bag to keep fingers kind of clean. Lick fingers to get every last drop of glaze. Enjoy! #GoTeam!

Maple Glaze

5. Blend all of the ingredients together. Set aside and start heating up the grill.

Homemade Chunky Applesauce

6. In a medium saucepan, melt the butter. Add the apples. Brown the apples in the butter. Add brown sugar to coat and caramelize the apples. Add water. Cover and bring to a boil. Reduce heat to low and simmer for approximately 10 minutes.

7. Add lemon juice. Stir until incorporated. Add cinnamon and nutmeg. Continue to cook for another 10 minutes or so. Once the mixture has softened, mash the mixture with a fork. Leave the apples chunky. Set aside to cool.

FRIED CHICKEN AND WAFFLES CUPCAKES

The recipe that I've included gives you the long way to make the recipe. It includes from-scratch chicken strips and muffins. No doubt making fresh fried chicken strips from scratch is a delicious way to make this treat. But, please note, you can skip the long way and substitute the fried chicken for store-bought strips. The wow! factor will win you fans far and wide, and the flavors will not be compromised as long as you get a great premade chicken strip. It's a muffin with fried chicken, waffles, and cream cheese frosting. So it may seem like a lot to pull this one together, but if you want the glory, you'll want to go for the gold. People will push other dishes aside when they see this coming.

Again, there are shortcuts you can take with this recipe. For example, you can purchase the fried chicken strips instead of making them from scratch. You can use a cornbread muffin mix instead of making them from scratch. And absolutely—you can buy the waffles. You can also buy premade cornbread muffins, if that makes life easier. I'm all about optimizing your time.

Makes 24 servings

Southern Fried Chicken Strips

2 lbs. chicken tenderloins

1 cup of peanut or vegetable oil

Marinade

1 cup buttermilk

2 Tbsp. Tabasco

2 tsp. fresh thyme leaves

1½ tsp. salt

¼ tsp. garlic powder

¼ tsp. paprika

¼ tsp. cayenne pepper

Breading

1½ cups flour

1 tsp. baking powder

1 tsp. kosher salt

¾ tsp. black pepper

¾ tsp. garlic powder

¾ tsp. paprika

¼ tsp. fresh thyme leaves

1 tsp. kosher salt

Muffins

24 cornbread muffins, baked in a ball jar using
    your favorite cornbread muffin mix

Maple Cream Frosting

1 cup quality maple syrup

¾ cup powdered sugar

½ lb. unsalted butter, at room temperature

2 tsp. vanilla extract

¼ tsp. kosher salt

⅛ tsp. cayenne pepper

⅛ tsp. smoked paprika

Garnish

24 (2-inch) pieces of fried chicken strips (from
    scratch or store-bought)

24 large cornbread muffins baked in 3-oz. ball jars

24 sprigs thyme

10 high-quality frozen waffles, toasted and
    quartered—you may have leftovers after
    quartering the waffles

maple syrup for drizzling

fried chicken

Southern Fried Chicken Strips

1. Place the chicken and marinade ingredients in a large plastic bag. Seal the bag. Shake well to coat the chicken. Refrigerate overnight, or for at least 5 hours.

2. Combine the breading ingredients in a medium bowl. Remove one piece of chicken from the marinade at a time. Press each piece of chicken into the breading, making sure to coat all sides. Place the breaded chicken on a wire grate (such as for cooling cookies) or on a parchment-covered platter in preparation for frying. Repeat with remaining pieces.

3. Line a baking sheet with paper towels. Add oil to a high-sided skillet about ¾-inch deep. Heat over high heat until the oil is gently rippling. Use tongs to place several strips of breaded chicken in the oil. Do not crowd the pan. Flip the frying chicken until all sides are golden, 4–5 minutes. Set cooked chicken on lined baking sheet to absorb oil. Fry remaining chicken in small batches.

Maple Cream Frosting

4. Combine all ingredients in the bowl of a stand mixer. Whisk on low until incorporated, about 1 minute. Increase speed to high and beat until frosting is light, about 3 minutes.

Assembly

5. You will need 24 (6-inch) wooden skewers to assemble the cupcakes. Frost the muffins. Fold a fried chicken strip in half and skewer it. Push it to the top of the skewer and add a piece of waffle below it. Press the skewer into the frosted cupcake. Stand a sprig of thyme alongside the skewer and drizzle a small amount of maple syrup over the skewered items, letting it drip onto the cupcake slightly.

THE HOT CHOCOLATE GRILL CUPCAKE

Another über-cute cupcake that is not only adorbs but a chocolatey dream boat. If you can serve these warm, they are unbelievable—but even cooled, they are a perfect treat. Set these on a mini grill as a serving tray along with the Cheeseburger Cupcakes.

Makes 24 servings

Hot Chocolate Grill Cupcake

¾ cup whipping cream

2 cups semisweet chocolate chips

1 box chocolate cake mix

1 box chocolate fudge instant pudding mix

1¼ cups water

½ cup coconut oil

3 eggs

Garnish

1 container dark chocolate frosting

50-60 Hot Tamales candies

black gel frosting with thin tip

1. In 1-quart saucepan, heat whipping cream over medium-high heat until hot, but not boiling. Stir in chocolate chips until melted and smooth. Refrigerate for 1 hour.

2. Heat the oven to 350 degrees.

3. Grease and flour 24 large muffin cups. Use a metallic or dark brown/black muffin liner. In a large bowl, beat the cake mix, pudding mix, water, oil, and eggs with hand mixer on low speed for about 2 minutes. Place ¼ cup of batter in each muffin cup. Spoon 1 tablespoon refrigerated chocolate mixture on top of batter in center of each cup.

4. Bake for 20 minutes. Let cool for 10 minutes. Frost with chocolate frosting. Garnish by drawing black grill grid on each cupcake and adding Hot Tamale candies as hot dogs on the "grill." Serve warm, if you can—if not, they are still great!

HOT WING CUPCAKES WITH BLUE CHEESE FROSTING

Haven't you always wanted to have your cake . . . and chicken wing, too? Here's your chance! These are sure to get a hungry conversation going, but once the noshing begins, you'll hear a hush followed by a faint yummmm. Then you'll see an empty platter, where 12 little Hot Wing Cupcake soldiers once stood at attention. Enjoy your moment of "tailgate-vittles-done-right" satisfaction!

Makes 12 servings

Chicken with Buffalo Hot Sauce

12 fresh mini chicken drumettes or wings

1 Tbsp. brown sugar

¼ cup hot sauce, plus ½ cup hot sauce reserved

¼ cup butter

Cornbread Cupcake

1 (8.5-oz.) package cornbread mix

¼ cup hot sauce

¼ cup blue cheese crumbles

¼ cup celery, finely diced

Blue Cheese Buttercream Frosting

3 oz. blue cheese, at room temperature

¾ cup butter

4 oz. cream cheese, at room temperature

1 cup powdered sugar

Garnish

12-14 small inner stalks of celery

12-14 (3-inch) carrot sticks

1 oz. blue cheese crumbles

1 oz. hot sauce, for drizzling

Chicken with Buffalo Hot Sauce

1. Preheat the oven to 425 degrees.

2. Arrange chicken on parchment-lined sheet pan. Mix together the brown sugar and ¼ cup hot sauce. Brush chicken pieces with it. Bake for 30 minutes or until the chicken is no longer pink in the center.

3. Combine the remaining ½ cup hot sauce and the butter in large bowl. Once the chicken is fully cooked, put the chicken into a large bowl. Mix with fresh hot sauce mixture to coat. Set aside.

Cornbread Cupcake

4. Make the cornbread batter, following the instructions on the package. Add hot sauce, blue cheese, and celery. Pour mixture into lined muffin tins. Follow baking times listed on the cornbread packaging. Once baked, set aside to cool completely.

Blue Cheese Buttercream Frosting

5. Mix the blue cheese on high speed until smooth. Add the unsalted butter and mix on high speed until fluffy.

6. Add room-temperature cream cheese. Mix in the powdered sugar slowly until fully incorporated.

Assembly and Garnish

7. Pipe or spread Blue Cheese Buttercream Frosting onto cooled Cornbread Cupcakes. Top frosted cupcake with fully cooked chicken wing or drumette (use a small skewer to attach to the cupcake).

8. Garnish with a small stalk of celery, a few crumbles of blue cheese, and a drizzle of hot sauce.

THE MEATLOAF CUPCAKE

Frosted with Mashed Potatoes, Sprinkled with Peas, Carrots, and BACON!

There's something so much fun about this cupcake. The merits are many! They're like your very own special treat. Bigger than a cookie yet smaller than a cake. They're the personal pan pizza of desserts. They can be eaten utensil free, and biting into that frosting is heavenly. And how cute are the sprinkles? But how about The Meatloaf Cupcake? Whoa! Mind blown! Could it be the most perfect portable meat-based bite in all of tailgate grub? You'll find a complete tailgate meal in this cupcake. It boasts four important tailgate staples: meat, potatoes, veggies, and . . . BACON! This recipe is truly a showstopper at any tailgate party!

Makes 12 servings

The Meatloaf Cupcake

1 lb. button or cremini mushrooms, finely diced

½ cup white onion, minced

½ cup butter, melted

4 cups soft breadcrumbs

½ tsp. thyme

1 bunch parsley leaves, minced

2½ lbs. 80/20 ground beef

3 eggs, slightly beaten

1½ tsp. salt

1 tsp. pepper

⅓ cup ketchup

Classic Mashed Potatoes (recipe below)

16 oz. cooked and buttered frozen peas

16 oz. cooked and buttered carrots, diced small

1 lb. crisp bacon crumbles

Classic Mashed Potatoes

5 pounds of Yukon Gold potatoes, peeled and cut into quarters

1 tablespoon salt

½ cup butter

½ cup heavy cream

4 oz. cream cheese

¼ cup milk

salt and pepper to taste

The Meatloaf Cupcake

1. Preheat the oven to 375 degrees.

2. Sauté the mushrooms and onion in butter until the onion is transparent. Combine with breadcrumbs, thyme, and parsley.

3. Lightly mix together the ground beef, eggs, salt, pepper, and ketchup. Add this mixture to the mushroom and onion mixture. Scoop three-fourths of the way up the lined muffin tin sections. Bake at 375 degrees for 1 hour and 15 minutes. Let stand for 10 minutes.

4. Your topping game is strong . . . Frost the cupcakes with the Classic Mashed Potatoes, and "sprinkle" them with peas, carrots, and bacon crumbles.

5. OR—this is where things can get DIY— set-up a little buffet, letting your fellow fans build their own Meatloaf Cupcake! Place your potatoes, peas, and carrots in mini-crockpots (yes, they have minis, and they are super cute) or warming dishes. Make sure to put the bacon crumbles in a ball jar or small bowl. Serve with spoons for sprinkling. Just like regular cupcakes, these meaty cupcakes can be messy. We're nothing if not civilized fans, even at the tailgate, right? . . . Napkin, anyone?

Classic Mashed Potatoes

6. Place the prepared potatoes in a medium pan. Add cold water until the water is 1 inch above the potatoes. Add 1 tablespoon of salt to the water.

7. Heat on high, and bring the water to a boil. Reduce the heat to low to maintain a simmer and cover. Cook for 15 minutes or until you can pierce the potatos with a fork.

8. While the potatoes are boiling and simmering, melt the butter and warm the heavy cream and cream cheese on low heat. You can heat them together in a pan on the stove on low heat (be careful not to scald the cream) or you can place them together in a small bowl in the microwave for 2 minutes.

9. Drain the potatoes and place them in a large bowl. Pour the warm cream and melted butter over the potatoes. Mash the potatoes with a potato masher. Stir with a wooden spoon to incorporate.

10. Add milk. Use a hand mixer to beat until the mashed potatoes are smooth. Don't over-beat the potatoes, or they will become glue-like, and nobody likes glue-y potatoes. Add salt and pepper to taste.

THE CHEESEBURGER BROWNIE CUPCAKE

How cute are these? Using a cake mix and a brownie mix makes this adorable cupcake far less complicated to create than it looks. It's actually pretty easy to make, but get ready for the ooohs and ahhhs! A super fun treat to bring to a tailgate. Decor tip: Find the smallest charcoal grill at your local hardware store—they have cute little mini ones. Once assembled, use it as your serving platter and amp up the cuteness factor! Folks will go wild over this presentation, plus, these are as tasty as they are cute!

Makes 12 servings

The Cheeseburger Brownie Cupcake

12 yellow cake cupcakes

12 (2-inch-round) brownies baked in muffin tins

Condiments (instructions below)

2 Tbsp. water

2 Tbsp. powdered sugar

Condiments

16 oz. store-bought buttercream frosting

food coloring gels, yellow and red

liquid food coloring, green

8 oz. sweetened flaked coconut

white sprinkles or little sprinkle balls

Special Equipment

2 decorating bags

12 skewers

The Cheeseburger Brownie Cupcake

1. Gently halve the cupcakes horizontally. Place the brownie burgers on the bottom halves of the cupcakes.

2. In a small bowl, stir the water and powdered sugar together. Set aside

3. Add the Condiments: Pipe the yellow buttercream frosting on top of the "burger" to look like cheese. Pipe the red buttercream frosting on top of the "cheese" to look like ketchup. Sprinkle the green coconut flakes on top of the ketchup to look like lettuce.

4. Place the top half of cupcake on top. Lightly brush the top of the cupcake with the powder sugar glaze. Immediately sprinkle the white sprinkles on top of the cupcakes to look like sesame seeds. Slide a skewer through the middle of the cupcake to hold the cupcake together for transporting.

Condiments

5. Mix half of the buttercream frosting with yellow food coloring, making the color of cheese. Spoon the frosting into a decorating bag.

6. Mix the other half of the buttercream frosting with red food coloring, making it the color of ketchup. Spoon the frosting into a decorating bag.

7. Mix the flaked coconut with liquid green food coloring, making it the color of lettuce.

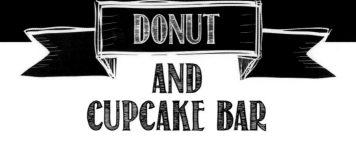

DONUT AND CUPCAKE BAR

Sugar, Candy, Cake, and Meatloaf, Oh My!

The Donut and Cupcake Bar is the thing of dreams. Willy Wonka wishes he had thought of this fantastical display of sugar cakes. Sugar Buzz = guaranteed!

Speaking of Willy Wonka . . . Remember when Violet Beauregard chews the gum that tastes like a three-course meal as she chews? Well, my savory cupcakes are kind of like that, without the side effect of turning you into a blueberry. Check out the mashed-potato-topped and hot-wing-topped cupcakes. Oh yeah, you heard me, mashed potatoes and hot wings on top of cupcakes—and there may even be a blue cheese frosting. I know, whoa!

Hey, Cupcake!

Get whimsical with this display. Use a mini grill as one of your serving pieces. You can find them at a local hardware store, hobby store, or online. It's a functional grill but mini, so it's super cute to use in this display for the Cheeseburger Brownie Cupcakes and Hot Chocolate Grill Cupcakes.

Sprinkles and Donuts!

I love colorful straws. They come in all different patterns—striped, polka dot, chevron, etc.—and in so many colors! They are great for sipping, but they also make perfect donut holders. I make a couple different donuts for my donut bar, but I also add more store-bought donuts. From donut holes to dozens of donuts. I skewer them and display. Add some Grilled Apple Cider Donuts and skewered donuts too!

Come on Down to My Candy Shop . . .

What would this sugar cake buffet be without some candy? Here's the scoop: Fill apothecary jars, mini buckets, and bowls with candy. Have all your buckets and bowls outfitted with scoops, and don't forget to include little bags for folks to use for filling. It's a feast of sweets that will be the talk of the parking lot!

The Savory Cupcake Bar

Whoa! Mind blown. A savory cupcake? Take a moment, sit down and wrap your brain around this amazing concept, and then give it a try! The beauty of this concept is that you get your four squares, a full meal, in one cupcake. Think about it . . . It's functional for a tailgate too. A compact one-handed meal. This is definitely not your mother's cupcake! The Meatloaf Cupcake, the Fried Chicken and Waffle Cupcake, and the super awesome Hot Wing Cupcake. It's a whole new way to cupcake!

THE DIY BAGGIE OMELETTE

The DIY Baggie Omelette is one of those genius make-ahead recipes that will rock your DIY brunch. On the night before or early morning of your tailgate, fill six half-quart Ziplock bags with the Omelette Base. Refrigerate. When you are ready to pack for the tailgate, place the bags and the DIY Ingredients in an icy cooler. To pack and then to display and serve the DIY ingredients, use the same sized Ziplock bags for transport. Bring fun containers, like ramekins or cute bowls to display and serve the DIY ingredients.

Here are a few things you will need to make this all work: Bring a medium-sized pot, water to fill the pan, a heating source—like a hot grill—a sharpie, and the DIY Ingredients setup. Don't forget little tongs or utensils set in or next to the DIY Ingredients containers so peeps can choose the ingredients that they want in their baggie. Next, folks grab a baggie full of the Omelette Base and start adding the DIY Ingredients. Then, mark the bag up with their name and pop it in the boiling water until the omelette is cooked through. Genius! Everyone will love their DIY Omelettes because it is "eggs"-actly what they wanted in it! And they get to have a warm and delicious omelette as they start their big game day tailgate . . . Plus, they will marvel at your gorgeous DIY Baggie Omelette Buffet! You are amazing!

Here's where things get fun. When you get to the tailgate, pop on the grill.

Makes 6 servings

Omelettes
1 dozen eggs (2 eggs per omelette)

Omelette Base (per omelette)
2 eggs
1 Tbsp. water
salt and pepper to taste
1 tsp. unsalted butter

DIY Ingredients
1 lb. white button mushrooms, prepared (instructions below)
3 red peppers, diced small
2 white onions, diced small

1 lb. cheddar cheese, shredded
½ lb. Swiss cheese, shredded
1½ lbs. spinach, prepared (instructions below)
½ lb. canadian bacon, diced
1 lb. bacon, cooked until crispy and crumbled
3 avocados, prepared (instructions below)
1 cup tomatoes, diced
½ cup broccoli, chopped

Extras
salsa
hot sauce
ketchup
Add whatever you think your crowd will love

Special Preparations for DIY Ingredients (optional)

Mushrooms

1½ Tbs. olive oil

1 lb. button mushrooms, cleaned and quartered

¼ tsp. minced garlic

kosher salt to taste

1. Saute over low-medium heat until mushrooms are soft and browned. iAbout 10 minutes.

Spinach

4 tsp. olive oil

2 tsp. minced garlic

1½ lbs. spinach

kosher salt to taste

2. Sauté over medium-low heat until spinach is wilted, about 5 minutes.

Avocados

3 ripe avocados, pitted and peeled

zest of ½ lemon

1 Tbs. fresh lemon juice

1 Tbs. finely chopped fresh chives

sea salt to taste

3. Blend gently, keeping avocados chunky.

DANISH EBLESKIVER WAFFLES

These cute little waffle bites are perfect for a tailgate. Make these ahead or bring the pan out to the tailgate and make them on the grill. They are dippable and perfect on a stick or skewered and then popped into a fun paper container. Check out all of the delicious ways you can serve the ebleskiver. Plus, it's just a super fun word to say . . . Ebleskiver, ebleskiver, ebleskiver! Ten times fast. P. S. You need an ebleskiver pan for this recipe, but they're easy to get on Amazon.com, William-Sonoma.com, Walmart. com, etc. The ebleskiver is everywhere. Stick with me, and I'll keep you ahead of waffle trends.

Makes 30 servings

1 cup flour

1 Tbsp. granulated sugar

2 tsp. baking powder

¼ tsp. salt

1 cup milk

2 egg yolks

2 egg whites

3 Tbsp. cooking oil

Additional Garnish

powdered sugar, sifted

cinnamon sugar mixture (equal parts cinnamon and sugar)

filling (your choice—jam, jelly, honey, syrup, chunky applesauce)

1. In a mixing bowl, combine flour, sugar, baking powder, and salt. In a separate bowl, mix the milk and egg yolks until well combined. Add the egg mixture to the flour and sugar mixture. Blend until smooth.

2. In a small bowl, beat the egg whites with a hand mixer on high until stiff peaks form. Gently fold the beaten egg whites into the batter. Do not overmix.

To Cook without Filling

3. Place an ebleskiver pan over medium heat. Brush each cup in the pan with oil. Pour 2 tablespoons of the batter in each cup, filling each ⅔ full. Cook for 2 minutes. Rotate the ebleskiver until they are golden brown and a toothpick inserted in their centers comes out clean.

To Cook with Filling

4. Place an ebleskiver pan over medium heat. Brush each cup in the pan with oil. Add a small amount of batter, and then add a teaspoon of filling. Then add batter to cover the filling. Continue to cook and rotate the ebleskiver until they are golden brown and a toothpick inserted in their centers comes out clean..

5. Sprinkle with powdered sugar/cinnamon sugar, and serve immediately.

DANISH

PANCAKES

WHIPPED CREAM

WAFFLE BITES

I'm going to make things really easy on you with these Waffle Bites. There will be no batter or waffle irons, no recipes to follow, no cooking at all—just warming. Here goes . . . Buy really nice frozen waffles (they have super high-quality ones in the frozen section—bypass the Eggos), take them home and bake them up, cut them in quarters, stack them in a lovely cloth-napkin-lined basket, set a ball jar filled with cute little skewers in the basket with the Waffle Bites, cover it all up with another cloth napkin, and transport it to the prettiest tailgate waffle bar. Set the basket next to the whipped cream, butter, syrup, etc., uncover the basket . . . and serve 'em up! Make some things, fake some things . . . It's called balance.

Makes approximately 24 drummettes

Raspberry Butter

Makes 10 servings

3 sticks unsalted butter, softened

2 Tbsp. powdered sugar

1 cup fresh raspberries

1. Add the softened butter and powdered sugar to a mixing bowl. Mix on high. Scrape down the sides of the bowl with a spatula. Add the fresh raspberries to the bowl. Gently stir them in. Stir until the berries break apart but are not smashed and burst.

2. Put the butter mixture onto a long sheet of plastic wrap set over a long sheet of foil. Wrap and roll the butter mixture into a log, twisting the foil ends. Chill for at least 2 hours until firm, and keep refrigerated until ready to use.

Homemade Whipped Cream

Makes 10 servings

1 cup heavy whipping cream, cold

4 Tbsp. powdered sugar

1 tsp. vanilla extract

1. Add the heavy cream, powdered sugar, and vanilla extract to the chilled mixing bowl. Using the whisk attachment, or in a large mixing bowl using a handheld mixer, mix on low speed. Increase the speed to medium-high, and mix until soft peaks form.

PRO TIP: *Place your mixing bowl and whisk attachment in the refrigerator or freezer for about 10-15 minutes to chill before starting the recipe.*

Maple Syrup Whipped Cream

Makes 10 servings

1 cup heavy whipping cream, cold

2 Tbsp. powdered sugar

2 Tbsp. high-quality maple syrup

1. Add the heavy cream, powdered sugar, and maple syrup to the chilled mixing bowl. Using the whisk attachment, or in a large mixing bowl using a handheld mixer, mix on low speed. Increase the speed to medium-high, and mix until soft peaks form.

PRO TIP FOR SERVING: *Treat the crew right and warm up their sweet little maple syrup. Fill a small slow-cooker with water, and place your maple syrup bottle in it for a nice warm bath. Set this on your DIY Waffle Bar for optimal waffle enjoyment.*

TOUCHDOWN BRUNCH

Midday games mean that tailgating needs to start early in the day. Honestly, it's one of my favorite kinds of game days. There is something so exciting about getting up and out early, the day holding so much promise for memory making. Football season is short—we need to make the most of every drop of game day and create a day to remember. What better way to kick it all off than with a tailgate brunch to rival all others? We need to celebrate each day. Tailgating with friends and family, serving up amazing food, sharing fun weekends throughout the football season . . . These are the joyous things that help us celebrate life. To celebrate your love for your team, community, family, and friends, set your tailgate party up for memory-making success. Looking for inspiration on how to bring all of that together? I've got you! Check out the Touchdown Brunch, including a DIY Waffle Bar, DIY Baggie Omelettes, Bloody Mary Jell-o Shots. (recipe on page 34)

Here is what you will find on the Touchdown Brunch Bar:

- DIY Waffle Bar (recipe on page 164)

- DIY Baggie Omelettes (recipe on page 156)

- The Bloody Mary Bar

TOUCHDOWN
BRUNCH
DIY WAFFLE BRUNCH BAR

Lay down a roll of black paper, one that is meant to be written on with a chalk pen, and get a chalk pen (you can get one at a hobby store). Showcase the brunch game plan by giving chalkboard directions on the paper. It's a neat thing to do, because you can determine where all your food will be displayed. If you know the size of the table and how you want to arrange things ahead of the tailgate, you can draw it all out at home, roll up the roll for transport, and unroll it for set-up when you get to the tailgate. This can also help you stay very organized, because it forces you to determine what serving dishes and food you will be displaying on the map you have created for the buffet.

Everything You Need for a Happy Touchdown Brunch DIY Waffle Brunch Bar

- pretty bowls
- spreading utensils
- skewers for stabbing, dipping, and holding waffles
- fun cloth napkins to line baskets full of waffles and their tasty accoutrements
- 2–3 pints berries, washed and served in the green pints from the market
- 1 cup Maple Syrup Whipped Cream (recipe on page 161)
- 1 cup Homemade Whipped Cream (recipe on page 160)
- ½ cup Raspberry Butter (recipe on page 160)
- 24 Danish Ebleskiver Waffles (recipe on page 158)
- 24 Skewered Waffles Bites (recipe on page 160)
- 3 different kinds of store-bought, high quality jellies & jams

. . . and you have yourself the best DIY Waffle Brunch Bar evah!

PRO TIP: Don't forget small spreading knives/spoons for the butter, the whipped cream, and jellies and jams. Arrows and X's and O's help the super-fan crew know what is what and what goes with what. After all, X's and O's make the world go around. Spread the love!

CHAPTER 7
END-ZONE DANCE

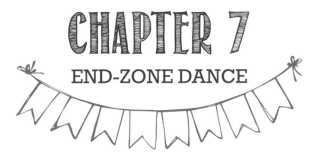

Game-Day Desserts

Desserts are easy to transport and with their fun-lovin' vibe, they pack a powerful presentation punch on a game-day spread. These handpicked treats will satisfy every kind of sweet tooth. If you are looking for creative and fun desserts, this chapter has them runnin' the ball and scootin' fast to the end zone. Shake it, baby—it's time for a victory dance!

CHERRY CREAM CHEESE HAND PIES

A Midwestern treat and great for the tailgate set. The dollop of cream cheese nestled under the pie filling makes these desserts flaky, & buttery. I suggest serving them warm from a small cooler bag. Warm them and wrap them in sheets of tin foil and pop them in the cooler bag before you head to the tailgate. They are so good when they're served warm at a cold tailgate.

Makes 24 servings

Cherry Cream Cheese Hand Pies

5 cups unbleached flour

2 tsp. kosher salt

2 Tbsp. granulated sugar

2 cups cold, unsalted butter, cut into ½-inch cubes

2 cups water, cold

½ cup apple cider vinegar

2 cups ice

Cream Cheese Filling (recipe below)

Cherry Filling (instructions below)

¼ cup heavy cream

raw or demerara sugar, for finishing

Cream Cheese Filling

4 oz. Philadelphia cream cheese, room temperature

¼ cup granulated sugar

zest of 1 lemon

1 egg yolk

Cherry Filling

16 oz. cherry pie filling

Cherry Cream Cheese Hand Pies

1. Stir the flour, salt, and sugar together in a large bowl. Add the butter cubes, and coat them with the flour mixture using a bench scraper or spatula. With a pastry blender, cut the butter into the flour mixture, working quickly, until mostly pea-sized pieces of butter remain.

2. Combine the water, vinegar, and ice in a large measuring cup or small bowl. Sprinkle ¼ cup of the ice-water mixture over the flour mixture. Mix and cut it in with a spatula until fully incorporated. Continue adding the ice-water mixture, 1 to 2 tablespoons at a time, mixing with your hands until the dough comes together in a ball with some dry bits remaining. Shape the dough into a flat disc, wrap it in plastic, and refrigerate it for at least 1 hour, to give the crust time to set.

Assemble and Bake

3. Preheat the oven to 350 degrees.

4. Roll chilled pie dough out on floured surface to ⅛-inch thickness. Use a cookie cutter to cut out 30–40 (4-inch) circles. Place a dollop of Cream Cheese Filling in the center of each of half of the circles. Top with a spoonful of Cherry Filling.

5. Cover with another pie-dough round. Gently pinch the edges together. Press the tines of a fork into the edge to seal further. Cut 2 small X-shaped slits evenly placed on the top of each pie with a sharp pairing knife.

6. Use a pastry brush to brush the tops with heavy cream and sprinkle with raw or demerara sugar. Chill in freezer for 10 minutes before baking. Bake 25–35 minutes, until golden brown.

Cream Cheese Filling

7. Combine all ingredients in the bowl of an electric mixer. Beat until smooth. Place Cream Cheese Filling in the fridge until ready to use.

Cherry filling

8. Pour the cans of filling in a small pan on the stove. Bring to a simmer for 5–7 minutes, until it has reduced a bit, stirring frequently. Let cool to room temperature.

JERRY JAMES STONE'S COCONUT, LIME, AND AVOCADO POPSICLES

Have you heard of my friend Jerry James Stone? If not, you gotta get out more, because this guy is everywhere! Jerry is a YouTube phenom and an inventive vegetarian food blogger. Find him first at jerryjamesstone.com, and then make your way around all of his other media. It's good stuff! He's a California boy bringing us a fresh take on this delicious, warm-weather tailgate dessert that will make you want to hula your team to victory! The tropical flavors of coconut and lime paired with that creamy avocado . . . Yum! Yum! All that goodness is blended up into a frozen-food-on-a-stick, and we like food on a stick at our tailgates. Here's a tip: Shades may be required as you enjoy this bite because it's just so bright!

Makes 10 servings

¾ cup granulated sugar

1 cup water

10 fresh tarragon leaves, chopped

2 extra-ripe avocados, peeled and pitted

juice of 2 limes, zest of 1 lime

1 cup coconut milk, plus ½ cup

1. Add the sugar and water to a small saucepan. Warm over medium heat until the sugar fully dissolves, about one minute. Remove from heat, and add the fresh tarragon. Cover and let steep for 3 minutes. Strain out the tarragon, reserving the liquid.

2. Add the avocados, lime juice and zest, 1 cup of coconut milk, and the tarragon-infused syrup to a food processor. Puree until smooth.

3. Divide the mixture among the popsicle molds, leaving a little room at the top. Carefully top off the avocado mixture with the remaining coconut milk.

4. Insert the popsicle sticks, and place the mold in the very back of the freezer. Freeze overnight for best results.

5. To remove the pops from the mold, fill your sink with tepid warm water (not hot!). Dip, but do not submerge, the mold in the water for about 10 seconds at a time, until you can easily wiggle out the popsicles loose. Don't force it.

6. The best way to bring these pops to a summer tailgate is to keep them frozen in their molds, packed in a cooler filled with ice.

EMILY ELLYN'S PEANUT BUTTER CARAMEL CHEESECAKE

This recipe was crafted by a true culinary genius, my friend, Chef Emily Ellyn. Not only is she a super smart culinarian, she is simply a delightful human being. If you look her up, you'll find her as the Retro Rad Chef and you may have spotted her on Food Network's Cupcake Wars, Next Food Network Star AND Cutthroat Kitchen. She's a food super-star, sporting fab cat rimmed glasses, retro dresses and kitchy aprons while mixing things up with her signature style of bringing fun to food with a retro twist. Oh, and everything she makes, not only fun but also delicious!

Makes 8–12 servings, depending on how you slice it

Peanut Butter Caramel Cheesecake

2 cups peanut butter puff cereal

1 cup caramel popcorn

5 Tbsp. unsalted butter, melted

Cheesecake Filling (recipe below)

Cheesecake Filling

12 oz cream cheese, room temperature

1½ cups whole-milk ricotta cheese

1½ cups creamy peanut butter

1 cup dulce de leche (or your favorite caramel sauce)

1 cup powdered sugar

½ tsp. pure vanilla extract

1 cup frozen whipped topping, room temperature

1 cup caramel popcorn, roughly chopped

Garnish

dulce de leche

caramel popcorn

peanut butter candies

honey roasted peanuts

Peanut Butter Caramel Cheesecake

1. Spray a 9-inch spring-form cake pan with cooking spray and line with parchment paper. Set aside.

2. In a food processor fitted with a blade, pulse peanut butter puff cereal, caramel popcorn, and butter until the mixture is pulverized into a thick, coarse, and sandy mixture. Press the mixture into the bottom of the lined spring-form cake pan.

3. Scrape Cheesecake Filling on top of crust. Smooth top with a pastry knife or back of a spoon and place in freezer. Freeze for at least 3 hours. Top as desired with dulce de leche, caramel popcorn, peanut butter cereal, and/or peanut butter candies and honey-roasted peanuts. Allow cake to slightly defrost, slice, serve, and enjoy!

Cheesecake Filling

4. In a large bowl mix together the cream cheese and ricotta cheese on high speed until soft and smooth, about 3 minutes. Add peanut butter, dulce de leche, powdered sugar, and vanilla extract. Whip until the mixture is thoroughly incorporated and smooth in texture, 3–5 minutes. On low speed, gently mix in the whipped topping until just incorporated.

S'MORES COOKIE SANDWICH

We all love our s'mores, but they can be a lot of work. Let's face it: it's hard to hold a drink while roasting a marshmallow! These premade S'mores Cookie Sandwiches are super convenient at the tailgate because they have all of the s'mores flavor and nostalgia but none of the burnt marshmallow drama. Since these treats are so delicious, who will keep an eye on the plate to make sure no one steals our sweets? You will need napkins for this treat!

Makes 10–12 servings

¾ cup butter, softened

½ cup sugar

½ cup packed brown sugar

2 eggs

1 tsp. vanilla extract

1¼ cups flour

1 cup graham cracker crumbs

½ cup chocolate graham cracker crumbs

½ tsp. baking soda

¼ tsp. salt

½ cup semi-sweet chocolate chips, or larger chunks

1 (6–8-oz.) jar marshmallow fluff

1. Preheat the oven to 375 degrees.

2. In a mixing bowl, cream the butter and sugars until light and fluffy. Beat in the eggs and vanilla. Add the flour, graham cracker crumbs, baking soda, and salt. Stir in the chocolate chunks.

3. Using a tablespoon, drop the dough 2 inches apart onto ungreased baking sheets. Bake for 8 minutes. Let cool.

4. Add a smear of (about a tablespoon) of marshmallow fluff to the bottom of one s'mores cookie and sandwich it with the bottom of another . . . *Voila!* You have a S'mores Cookie Sandwich! I suggest you freeze these and keep them in a cooler to thaw prior to serving at your campfire soiree!

HONEYCRISP APPLE PANNA COTTA

Definitely put this on your "honey do" list! It's an autumn tailgate dessert extraordinaire. Honeycrisp apples are at their peak in the fall, and you can make these creamy delights in ball jars. Perfect for packing in the cooler and transporting to the parking lot. Panna cotta seems sophisticated, and yes, it is beautiful enough for a fancy culinary company, but it is basically an Italian comfort food of pudding with a little Jell-O and granola on top. Make enough for the kids—they will gobble it up.

Makes 10 servings

Honeycrisp Apple Panna Cotta

3½ cups whole milk

3 cups heavy cream

¾ cup sugar

2 vanilla beans, split and scraped

4 cinnamon sticks, broken

1 Tbsp. butter

1 large Honeycrisp apple, peeled and finely diced

3 tsp. unflavored gelatin

¼ cup water, cold

Apple Cider Gelee (recipe below)

Cinnamon Toasted Granola and Apple Crumble (recipe below)

Apple Cider Gelee

(make while panna cotta is setting)

3 cups Honeycrisp apple cider (or regular apple cider)

3 Tbsp. sugar

1 tsp. gelatin

1 Tbsp. water, cool

Cinnamon Toasted Granola and Apple Crumble

3 Tbsp. of your favorite granola

1 tsp. butter

1 Tbsp. Honeycrisp apple cider (or apple cider)

1 tsp. honey

1 tsp. ground cinnamon

reserved sautéed Honeycrisp apple pieces

Honeycrisp Apple Panna Cotta

1. Pour the milk and cream in a medium saucepan. Add the sugar, split vanilla beans, and cinnamon sticks. Bring to a simmer, stirring slowly throughout. Remove from heat, and cover the pan. Let it sit for about 20 minutes. Strain the cinnamon and vanilla beans from the liquid. Pour the liquid back into the pan.

2. On medium-low heat, melt 1 tablespoon of butter in a sauté pan. Add the diced apple. Sauté until softened and light brown. Remove from heat and let cool.

3. In a small bowl, sprinkle 3 teaspoons of unflavored gelatin over ¼ cup of cold water. Let it sit for 2 minutes. Spoon the gelatin into the saucepan with the vanilla-cream mixture and whisk together. Pour the mixture into 10 medium ball jars, filling each ¾ full.

4. Refrigerate for 2 hours. Keep the jars uncapped while the panna cotta is setting, but make sure you have lids for each jar—you will use them when transporting the panna cotta. Once the mixture is set, top each jar with ½ teaspoon of the sautéed apple pieces. Set the remaining apple pieces aside to be used in the Cinnamon Toasted Granola and Apple Crumble. Refrigerate for another 2 hours.

5. Make sure you have a nice skin on the panna cotta. Gently pour ¼ inch (about 2 Tbsp.) of the Apple Cider Gelee over a spoon over each of the panna cotta jars, being careful not to break the skin. Refrigerate for 2 more hours. Top with Cinnamon Toasted Granola and Apple Crumble. Place a cap on each jar, and pack the jars in an icy cooler to bring to the parking lot.

Apple Cider Gelee

6. Add the cider and sugar to a saucepan. Let boil and reduce for 15 minutes. Sprinkle the gelatin over the cool water. Let it sit for 2 minutes. Whisk the gelatin into the cider until dissolved. Pour the liquid into a measuring cup. Let it cool for 20–30 minutes.

Cinnamon Toasted Granola and Apple Crumble

7. In a medium sauté pan, toast the granola in melted butter. Add the cider, honey, and cinnamon. Stir in the remaining sautéed Honeycrisp apple pieces until incorporated, warm the mixture, stirring periodically, for 2 more minutes, then, remove from heat Pour onto a parchment sheet so the mixture does not clump. Let the mixture set for at least 1 hour to cool, then, with your hands, crumble the mixture over the set panna cotta.

KILLER CHUNK CHOCOLATE CAKE WITH CHOCOLATE BUTTERCREAM FROSTING

I do not encourage chocolate at a tailgate unless it's chilly out because melty! melty! melty! *Our beloved chocolate can be such a hot mess. Make this cake when the temperatures have fallen and the melt factor isn't a thing. It's not a fancy cake, but it's easy to make, transport, and serve, and folks will love it. The cinnamon mayonnaise makes this cake something special. Classic case of "Don't judge a book by its cover." It's moist, buttery, and chocolatey, and it's a from-scratch cake, so appreciation will abound.*

Makes 10 servings (or one, if I'm alone with it)

Killer Chunk Chocolate Cake

2 cups flour

⅔ cup unsweetened cocoa

½ lb. dark chocolate chunks

1 tsp. baking soda

¼ tsp. salt

¼ tsp. baking powder

3 large eggs

1½ cups packed brown sugar

2 tsp. vanilla extract

1 cup Cinnamon Mayo (recipe below)

1½ cups hot water

Cinnamon Mayo

1 cup mayonnaise

2 Tbsp. cinnamon

2 Tbsp. sugar

Chocolate Buttercream Frosting

6 Tbsp. butter, softened

2⅓ cups confectioners' sugar

½ cup cocoa

⅓ cup milk

1½ tsp. vanilla

Killer Chunk Chocolate Cake

1. Preheat the oven to 350 degrees. Grease (with shortening) and flour a 9" × 13" pan.

2. In a medium bowl, whisk together the flour, cocoa, chocolate chunks, baking soda, salt, and baking powder. Beat the eggs, sugar, and vanilla at medium-high speed with a heavy-duty electric stand mixer about 3 minutes, or until the mixture is very light brown and ribbons form when the beater is lifted. Add mayonnaise, and beat at low speed until combined.

3. Add the flour mixture to the egg mixture alternately with hot water, beginning and ending with the flour mixture and beating at low speed just until blended after each addition.

4. Pour the batter into the prepared pan. Bake for 30–35 minutes, until a wooden pick inserted in center comes out clean. Cool completely on a wire rack (about 1 hour). Frost the cake with the Chocolate Buttercream Frosting.

Cinnamon Mayo

5. In a medium bowl, fold the ingredients together.

Chocolate Buttercream Frosting

6. Place the butter in a bowl. Beat with a mixer until creamy. Add the sugar and cocoa. Mix well. Stir in the milk. Add the vanilla, and mix until combined.

MINI APPLE PIES IN A JAR

Tailgating is as American as apple pie! These little lovelies are easy to make, easy to transport, and easy to eat. What a happy delight for all your fellow tailgaters!

Makes 10 servings

zest of 1 lemon

2 Tbsp. lemon juice

¼ tsp. cinnamon

2 premade pie crusts (these often come in packages of 2)

8 oz. shredded cheddar cheese

2 8 oz cans apple pie filling

1 egg white, beaten for egg wash

1. Preheat the oven to 425 degrees.

2. In a medium pan, warm the pie filling, lemon juice, and ¼ teaspoon of cinnamon. Bring the mixture to a simmer. Set aside.

3. To prepare the crust, remove the premade dough from the package and lay the crusts, separately, on a sheet of parchment. Roll them out, stretching the dough to about ⅛ of an inch thick and 3 inches in diameter. Sprinkle one of the pieces of rolled dough with the cheese. Cover the cheddar with the other piece of dough. Use a rolling pin to flatten the dough until it is one piece. Take one of the tops of the ball jars (the metal ring) and cut 10 round pieces of cheese-filled dough.

4. Place 10 mini ball jars on a parchment-lined sheet pan. Spoon the apple filling mixture into the jars. Place the round dough cutouts over the top of the jars and pinch the dough to the rim of the jar. Cut three small slits to vent the jars. Brush the pastry top with the beaten egg white.

5. Bake the pies in the jars on the sheet pan for 25 minutes. Let them cool. Then tie a fork around each pie with kitchen twine or a ribbon of your team's colors.

PEACH BREAD WITH CHEDDAR CRUMBLE

Morning tailgate food sets the crew on the right path for the entire day because tailgate mornings lead into long afternoon games and fun nights. All of that action requires carb-o-licious tummy-fillers like this one. The Peach Bread can easily be made ahead of time and packaged up for game day.

Makes 10 servings

Peach Bread

2 packages crescent dough, rolled out to
⅛-inch thickness

Grilled Peaches (recipe below)

Cream Cheese and Peach Filling
(recipe below)

Cheddar Crumble (recipe below)

Maple Cream Sauce (recipe below)

Cream Cheese and Peach Filling

1 (8-oz.) package cream cheese, softened

¼ cup fresh mint, chiffonade

2 Tbsp. confectioners' sugar

½ tsp. almond extract

Grilled Peaches (see recipe below)

Grilled Peaches

½ cup unsalted butter, room temperature

1 tsp. cinnamon sugar (2 parts sugar to 1
part cinnamon or an already mixed blend
from the grocery store)

2 Tbsp. brown sugar

a pinch of salt

8 ripe peaches, halved and pitted

Cheddar Crumble

½ cup brown sugar

1 cup flour

1 tsp. cinnamon

½ cup walnuts, chopped

¼ cup shredded cheddar cheese

⅔ cup unsalted butter, chilled and diced

Maple Cream Sauce

1 cup heavy whipping cream

1 Tbsp. brown sugar

remaining cinnamon-butter mixture

1 Tbsp. Maple syrup

PRO TIP: *If it's easy to grill the peaches at home, great. If not, this can be made by instead cooking the peaches in a cast-iron skillet or regular sauté pan.*

Peach Bread

1. Preheat the oven to 375 degrees.

2. Roll the two packages of crescent rolls into a 9"× 5" inch greased loaf pan . Place the Cream Cheese and Peach Filling in the center of the bread.

3. Fold up all sides of the bread, leaving a long center opening, exposing the filling of the bread.

4. Pour the Maple Cream Sauce to the top of the bread prior to baking. Sprinkle the prepared Cheddar Crumble to the top of the bread. Bake the bread for 11–14 minutes or until golden brown.

Cream Cheese and Peach Filling

5. In a medium bowl, mix together all of the filling ingredients except peaches. Then gently incorporate the chopped Grilled Peaches.

Grilled Peaches

6. Preheat the grill to high.

7. In a small bowl, add the melted butter, cinnamon, brown sugar, and salt. Stir until combined. Brush the peaches with cinnamon-butter mixture Reserve the remaining cinnamon-butter mixture for the Maple Cream Sauce. Grill the peaches on high until golden brown and just cooked through. Dice the grilled peaches.

Cheddar Crumble

8. Combine all ingredients in food processor except butter. Add butter a few pieces at a time, and pulse until incorporated into a dry crumble, that can hold its shape when pressed together.

Maple Cream Sauce

9. In a small saucepan, combine the whipping cream and butter. Add the remaining cinnamon-butter mixture from the Grilled Peaches instructions. Cook on medium heat, stirring occasionally until the sauce has thickened.

10. Add maple syrup, and cook for about 2 minutes, stirring constantly.

THE 50/50 BAR

The lemon bar is one of those humble desserts so simple and fresh that it may get forgotten for a moment when placed next to something seemingly more decadent, like chocolatey dessert. But fret not, the lemon bar is never truly forgotten because a plate of them is like an old friend. As soon as they land on the tailgate table, smiles come and you hear indiscriminate whispers of "Who brought the lemon bars?" Just when we thought the good ol' lemon bar could not be improved, a hot new take, The 50/50 Bar, enters the scene. It climbs the citrus charts, made with not just lemon but lime, too. Pucker up for a sweet citrus punch to the kisser!

Makes 14–16 bars

The 50/50 Bar

1 cup soft butter
2 cups flour
½ cup sugar
zest of 2 lemons, reserve half for garnish
zest of 2 limes, reserve half for garnish
Soda Pop Lemon Curd (see recipe below)
Soda Pop Lime Curd (see recipe below)
confectioners' sugar, for garnish

Soda Pop Lemon Curd

3 large eggs
½ cup sugar
¼ cup fresh lemon juice
zest of 1 large lemon
4 Tbsp. cold butter, diced
⅛ cup lemon-lime soda

Soda Pop Lime Curd

3 large eggs
½ cup sugar
zest of 1 large lime
¼ cup fresh lime juice
4 Tbsp. cold butter, diced
⅛ cup lemon lime soda

The 50/50 Bar

1. Preheat the oven to 350 degrees.

2. Pulse all of the ingredients in a food processor 4 or 5 times, for 5 seconds each time, until the dough holds together. Press the dough evenly into the bottom of an ungreased 9" × 13" pan.

3. Gently press the tines of a fork into the dough in three rows. Bake for 20 minutes, until crust is raised slightly and golden brown.

4. Make the Soda Pop Lemon Curd and Soda Pop Lime Curd while the crust is cooling.

5. Once the crust and curds have cooled, spoon one layer of the Soda Pop Lemon Curd on the crust, and smooth the top. Spread the Soda Pop Lime Curd on top. Shake a light dusting of powdered sugar and a light sprinkle of lemon and lime zest over the top.

6. Refrigerate for 1 hour. Cut the bars into 2-inch squares. If you are heading to a warm-weather tailgate, keep this dessert cold until right before serving.

Soda Pop Lemon Curd and Soda Pop Lime Curd

7. In a medium bowl, add the ingredients for the lemon curd except the butter. Whisk until smooth.

8. Pour the liquid into a medium saucepan over medium heat. Stir constantly with a wooden spoon until the curd thickens, about 7 minutes. Reduce the heat to low, and add the butter. Stir until smooth.

9. Pour into a medium bowl. Cover and refrigerate for at least 1 hour. Repeat with lime curd ingredients to make the lime curd.

THE SLURPING WATERMELON

The Slurping Watermelon is two parts fresh summer fruit salad and one part sips of citrusy sweetness. The fresh brightness of the lime juice mixed with the sweet watermelon and herbalicious mint makes for a crisp combo at a warm early-season tailgate gathering. The best part: transporting and serving is a breeze when you break out the mini ball jars and give everyone their very own. With a team-colored twine or ribbon, attach all of the needed utensils, like a plastic or wooden fork and a straw for that double-time enjoyment. Make these gems ahead of time and place them in an iced-down cooler for transport and to keep chilled at the party. These should be served icy cold for optimal refreshment. Only 4 ingredients, including watermelon, lime juice, honey, and mint. Delicious and refreshing!

Makes 6–10 servings

1 large watermelon, rind removed, diced into 1-inch cubes

4 limes, juiced

¼ cup honey

1 bunch mint leaves, chiffonade, reserve ⅛ of the bunch for garnish

a sprinkle of high-quality salt (optional)

a sprinkle of cayenne pepper (optional)

1. In a large bowl, gently toss all of the ingredients.

2. Scoop the mixture into jars (with lids) that are small enough to be individual servings for the guests. Close the top and place the jars on ice in your cooler. Attach a fork and straw with kitchen twine to each jar so that you can easily pull them out of the cooler and have them ready to bite and slurp!

CHAPTER 8

ALL AMERICAN

Tailgate Recipes from around the Country

You do you, USA! Because you're awesome.

Like I mentioned in chapter 1, a few years back I had that lucky gig with Sam's Club and Coke Zero as a professional tailgater at more than twenty ESPN game days. My job was to basically be a tailgate guest. My only task was to eat delicious tailgate food at every tailgate around the country. I did my job well and ate a ton of wings, sliders, ribs, brisket, pulled pork, cheesy potatoes, and a lot more. It was an extraordinary experience for a lot of reasons, but one unexpected experience struck me as I bopped from bite to bite around the country. I won't forget the moment I realized the cool factor on the differences of tailgate food based on region. I was in Eugene, Oregon, at a University of Oregon vs. Michigan State game. One minute, I was standing in the UO tailgate enjoying a fresh-caught Pacific salmon served off a hot tailgate grill while sipping a crisp Oregon sauvignon blanc. Lovely. Next, I walked across the field to a Michigan State tailgate. The MSU menu skewed very Midwestern—I was offered a Polish sausage and sauerkraut and ultimate mac n' cheese, all to be washed down with a stacked Bloody Mary. Each menu was so regionally focused, showcasing the comfort foods of their parts of the country. I felt like I got a master class in American food cultures and communities through the flavors presented at each tailgate I was fortunate enough to be an honored eater at.

Kinda heady for tailgate grub? I don't know, I think it's a pretty cool study on the US of A. Such an authentic way to experience the true essence of our country. It's one thing to vacation somewhere and enjoy regions from a tourist point of view, but to be in it, with the locals, enjoying their happy hospitality, having them cook their regional comfort food for you . . . Well, that experience is a gift. So much so that it motivated me to add this entire chapter featuring several regional favorites and recipes that were inspired by specific parts of our great country. If you want a Cajun taste sensation, I've got your covered. If you want a warm Norwegian soup, you are all set. If you're looking to impress with the stylings of a deep south alligator recipe, look no further. From north to south, east to west, and all points in between, you are good to go! #GoUSA with all your uniquely "you" food.

SOUTHERN SWEET TEA

Like red wine is to Italy, Guiness to Ireland, sweet tea is to the South. It's less of an addiction but more of an obsession in the South. I hardly think that the rest of the world understands or appreciates how much southerners love their sweet tea—it's served with most southern meals. Much to the chagrin of aficionados, you can back off the sugar a bit and it will still be plenty sweet.

Makes 7–12 servings

3 cups water

2 family-size tea bags

1 cup sugar (or less if desired)

7 cups cold water

1. Bring 3 cups of water to a boil in a saucepan. Add the tea bags. Boil for 1 minute, and then remove from heat. Cover and steep 10 minutes. Remove and discard tea bags. Add sugar, stirring until dissolved. Pour into a 1-gallon container. Add 7 cups cold water. Serve over ice.

For Lemonade Sweet Tea:

2. Stir together 2 quarts Southern Sweet Tea made with ½ cup sugar. Add 1 cup thawed lemonade concentrate. Stir well. Serve over ice. Makes 2¼ quarts.

For Peach Sweet Tea:

3. Stir together 1½ quarts Southern Sweet Tea made with ½ cup sugar. Add 1 (8-oz.) bottle peach nectar and ¼ cup lemon juice. Stir well. Serve over ice. Makes 2½ quarts.

WHITNEY'S GATOR CORNDOGS

This fun recipe is from my pal Whitney Miller. She's the very first winner of Fox's MasterChef, she's from Mississippi, and she knows tailgate food! #GoGatorCorndogs! This is a message below from her about the recipe. I've made this recipe, and if you haven't had gator, don't be afraid—it tastes like chicken.

Gator is one of those meats that either you love or are afraid to try. To those of you who love gator meat, there is no convincing involved because you are willing and ready to bite into these delectable corndogs. To those of you who are on the fence, take the step and make my gator corndog the best first bite of gator you will ever try. The blend of the pork with the gator provides your palate familiarity in the flavor of the sausage.

So, its game day and you are thinking, What should I make for tailgating? Look no further than these tasty Gator Corndogs. Your tailgating guests will definitely be impressed with the food, but don't forget presentation as well. To serve, fill a deep bowl or cute bucket with grits or corn and then stick your corn dog sticks in to stand. Serve the sauces in individual bowls or mini mason jars for easy dipping. Now the rest of the decor is up to you, but for my husband's family, it's orange and blue! —Chef Whitney Miller

Makes 12 servings

Whitney's Gator Corndogs

2 lbs. ground gator/pork sausage***

1 cup flour *

1 cup yellow cornmeal

3 Tbsp. granulated sugar

1 tsp. baking powder

½ tsp. baking soda

½ tsp. fine sea salt

1 Tbsp. unsalted butter

1½ cups whole buttermilk

1 large egg

canola oil for frying

Honey Mustard (recipe below)

Remoulade (recipe below)

Honey Mustard

½ cup coarse ground Dijon mustard

2 Tbsp. honey

½ tsp. yellow mustard

Remoulade

½ cup mayonnaise

3 tsp. ketchup

2 tsp. fresh ground horseradish **

½ tsp. coarse ground Dijon mustard

½ tsp. fresh lemon juice

¼ tsp. cayenne pepper

a pinch of cracked black pepper

salt to taste

* For a gluten-free version, substitute gluten-free all-purpose flour.

** Find the fresh ground horseradish in a jar in the refrigerator section of the grocery store.

*** Substitute your favorite sausage like andouille, chicken, etc.

Whitney's Gator Corndogs

1. Creating one sausage link at a time, layer two medium-size pieces of plastic wrap on the kitchen counter. Measure ⅓ cup of the sausage and form into a 4½-inch log, by rolling it in your hands.

2. Place the sausage in the middle of the two layers of plastic wrap and tightly roll the sausage link in the plastic. Twist the ends tightly and tie a tight knot with the plastic at each end. Set aside and repeat with the plastic wrap and additional sausage to make 12 sausage links altogether.

3. Bring a large saucepan full of water to a boil. Place the sausages in the boiling water and cook for 4½ minutes. Transfer the sausage links to a baking sheet with tongs. Allow to cool at room temperature for 10 minutes, and then cut the plastic knot off each end of the sausage links and remove the plastic.

4. Preheat a charcoal grill to 300 degrees.

5. Grill the sausage links over indirect heat for 8 minutes on each side. Allow to cool for 10 minutes and then store in a zip-top bag. Refrigerate for at least 2 hours, or overnight.

6. To prepare the batter, combine the flour, cornmeal, sugar, baking powder, baking soda, and salt in a medium bowl.

Melt the butter in a small bowl. Add the melted butter and buttermilk to the dry ingredients. Whisk to combine. Add the egg, and whisk until smooth.

7. Pour the oil in a large heavy pot, and heat to between 365 and 375 degrees.

8. Insert a bamboo skewer into each sausage link two-thirds of the way through. Working with half of the sausage links at a time, dip each sausage link into the batter and allow excess to drip off for a second. Immediately drop into the oil. Using tongs, pinch the skewer to flip the corn dogs around while cooking for even browning. Cook until browned, about 3 minutes.

9. Transfer to a cooling rack to drain for a couple minutes. Repeat the process with the additional sausage links. Serve the Gator Corn Dogs with the Honey Mustard and Remoulade dipping sauces.

Honey Mustard

10. Combine the Dijon mustard, honey, and yellow mustard in a small bowl. Stir until smooth.

Remoulade

11. Combine the mayonnaise, ketchup, horseradish, mustard, lemon juice, cayenne pepper, and black pepper in a small bowl. Stir until smooth. Season with salt to taste.

THE EAST

THIS IS WHERE IT ALL BEGAN, IN THE EAST. Football in the East is full of history. Dare I say, much of the fanfare and tradition that is spread throughout the country related to football and tailgating began with the college football celebrations in the East. Afterall, the first real football tailgate happened about 145 years ago, in 1869, at the first college football game held between Rutgers and Princeton. The story goes that they grilled sausages in the field next to the football field. No car tailgates; they were partying at the back end of horses' tails. Fortunately, we have made serious strides when it comes to partying in the parking lot. From sausages over the coals to Philly cheesesteaks served up Philly proud. That's some delish progress!

VV'S PHILLY CHEESESTEAK SLIDERS

They are dead serious about their Philly cheesesteaks in Philly. This is my childhood BFF's game-time appetizer. She lives in Dover, Delaware, close enough to Philly that she has an authentic version of her own. Overall, I would rate the sandwiches on the East Coast as some of the best ever, and coming from a midwesterner, that's saying a lot. The other thing I like about Philly is the movie Invincible—The Vince Papali Story. *With two boys, I've found that football movies are a standard element of most of my weekends. We have watched it so many times I was forced to fall in love with the Philadelphia Eagles classic. Make these sliders and watch the movie, and remember, napkins may need to run double-duty because* Invincible *is a tear-jerker. "Are you crying again, Mom?" "Ohhh . . . I think it's the onions in the VV slider, boys . . . sniff, sniff. Pass me a napkin, please."*

Makes 12 servings

12 Hawaiian rolls

4 ribeye or top sirloin steaks, thinly sliced (about 2 lbs. total)

salt and pepper to taste

4 Tbsp. butter, divided

1 green pepper, diced

2 onions, one sliced, one minced

1 lb. white button mushrooms, sliced

3 Tbsp. mayonnaise

1 can Cheez Whiz

6 slices provolone cheese, halved

1. Preheat the oven to 350 degrees.

2. Separate the tops and bottoms of your rolls, and place the bottoms in an 11" × 7" casserole dish. In a medium skillet on medium heat, cook the thinly sliced steak meat quickly (2 minutes per side), adding salt and pepper to taste.

3. Remove the steak from the pan, and set it aside. In the same (unwashed) pan, melt 2 Tbsp. of butter. Sauté the green pepper, sliced onion, and mushrooms until soft. Set aside.

4. In a smaller skillet, add the remaining 2 Tbsp. of butter, sauté the minced onions. Remove from heat. Set aside.

5. Prep the bread by spreading a thin layer of mayonnaise on the tops and bottoms of the rolls.

6. Pile the steak, peppers, mushrooms, and onions evenly over the bottom pieces of bread in the casserole dish.

7. Squirt about 1 squirt of canned cheese over the top of each sandwich's pepper mixture. Top with a slice of provolone cheese. Place the top pieces of bun on top of the cheese. Brush the tops of the bun with a mix of melted butter and sautéed diced onions.

8. Cover with foil and bake for 10 minutes. Remove foil and continue baking for another 10 minutes (or until cheese is melted). Cut and serve.

THE MIDWEST

LIKE THE PEOPLE, THE COMFORT FOOD IN THE MIDWEST IS STURDY. We are a tough bunch in the center of the country as we endure some of the more inclement weather in this country with those famous, very cold winters. Our tailgates, the ones later in the season, can be darn-right unbearably freezing cold. Wind, rain, snow, and negative temperatures rarely keep the diehards from packing it all up, bundling up, and getting out into the elements to eat their casseroles, soups, chili, and really anything with beef in it . . . Oh, and . . . ya know, to celebrate their team. The meat-and-potato, stick-to-your-ribs stereotype is rooted deep in truth. Check this out . . . I grew up in the Midwest with a Sicilian mom. Her father was a fisherman in Sicily, and for a time, in Monterey, California. Sicily is surrounded by the ocean, so fish is an important part of the Sicilian diet. My mom, despite her heritage and her father's long-time profession, grew up in the Midwest and . . . hated fish. I, in turn, grew up never eating fish because she never, ever served it. She was a great cook, don't get me wrong, but we ate a lot of roast beef, steaks, pork roast, and . . . mashed potatoes. That made her Irish/Midwestern mother-in-law very happy. I've included a casserole and my favorite tailgate sandwiches, and, sorry as it should be, no fish. The Chicago Italian Beef Sandwich is a staple at the Midwestern tailgate, especially in my family. Enjoy!

BACON CHEESEBURGER TATER TOT SHEPHERD'S PIE

In the Midwest, if casseroles are king, then burgers are everything else. The fact is it's cold for a lot of the tailgate season in the Midwest, and comfort food warms—not just the soul, but bellies, too. Just like the center of the country, this dish is warm, familiar, and friendly. One bite of this cozy casserole will bring you to the heart of all things comfort. Warning: naps are a likely result of this yummy snuggle bite.

Makes 6–8 servings

Bacon Cheeseburger Tater Tot Shepherd's Pie

1 (32-oz.) bag frozen tater tots

2 lbs. lean ground beef

1 cup white onion, chopped

2 garlic cloves, minced

1 (6-oz.) can tomato paste

1 cup water

1 cup frozen corn

1 cup frozen peas

½ cup dill pickles, diced

½ cup grainy mustard

1½ cups shredded cheddar cheese

Mashed Potatoes (recipe below)

½ bunch green onions, sliced, for garnish

½ lb. crispy bacon crumbles, for garnish

Mashed Potatoes

2 lbs. potatoes

½ cup sour cream

½ cup butter

½ cup cheese

½ cup milk

1 tsp. salt

Bacon Cheeseburger Tater Tot Shepherd's Pie

1. Preheat the oven to 350 degrees.

2. In a long, deep casserole dish, bake tater tots per instructions, but underbake by 5 minutes. This will be the base of the dish. Once the tots are baked, set them aside.

3. In a large skillet, brown the beef, onion, and garlic over medium heat. Drain the grease. Stir in the tomato paste, water, corn, peas, pickles, and mustard. Bring to a simmer, uncovered, and let simmer for 5 minutes. Stir in ½ cup cheese. Remove from heat.

4. Spoon the beef mixture into the baking dish with the tater tots. Spoon the Mashed Potatoes in large scoops over the beef mixture. Sprinkle with the remaining cheese. Bake about 20 minutes—the cheese will be melted. Garnish with green onions and bacon.

Mashed Potatoes

5. In a large pan, boil the potatoes in salted water until tender. Drain. Mash with an electric mixer on low. Add sour cream, butter, cheese, milk, and salt. Do not overbeat the potatoes. They should be light and fluffy.

SLOW COOKER CHICAGO ITALIAN BEEF SANDWICHES

Now let me present the Chicago Italian Beef Sandwiches, near and dear to my heart. Don't miss out on topping this Chicago-authentic sandwich with the seasoned sweet sautéed green peppers and the classic giardiniera! Giardiniera seems to be a regional condiment. If you haven't had giardiniera peppers, they are pickled veggies and peppers that are packed in olive oil. So delicious! Also, the sandwiches are meant to be juicy—I encourage ladling some of the juice to each sandwich when serving.

Makes 12 servings

Slow Cooker Chicago Italian Beef Sandwiches

4 lbs. chuck roast

2 cups beef broth

1 (16-oz.) jar sliced Pepperoncini peppers, drained

1 Tbsp. dried oregano

1 tsp. dried basil

1 tsp. onion powder

1 tsp. garlic powder

1 tsp. black pepper

2 garlic cloves, minced

1 Tbsp. salt

12 full-size hoagie or Italian rolls

1 (6-oz.) jar Italian giardiniera, for topping

Green Pepper Sauté

1 Tbsp. olive oil

3 sweet green peppers, seeded, trimmed, and sliced into large slices

¼ tsp. oregano

1 tsp. garlic powder

salt and pepper to taste

Slow Cooker Chicago Italian Beef Sandwiches

1. Add all ingredients from the chuck roast through the salt to the slow cooker, and set on high. Cook 4–5 hours or until easily shredded. Once the beef easily pulls apart, shred the beef directly in the slow cooker with two forks.

2. Load rolls with meat. Top with Green Pepper Sauté and giardiniera, and enjoy!

Green Pepper Sauté

3. Heat the olive oil in a pan. Add the green peppers, oregano, garlic powder, salt, and pepper. Sauté until soft.

THE NORTH

IN FARGO, NORTH DAKOTA, at the North Dakota State University tailgate, slabs of grilled beef tenderloin with a side bowl of a hearty potato-and-meat Norwegian stew called *Lapskaus* was on the menu. The hot soup sat in one or two slow cookers and was proudly present at every single tailgate tent. I say tent, and yes, there were tents as I entered, but the tents quickly led to what I would call mini compounds all dedicated to the art of fine tailgate entertaining. The tents led us into a maze of larger insulated makeshift structures. As we walked deeper into a tailgate party, the insulated structures shielded us from the windy, freezing cold temperatures that hit that part of the country early in tailgate season. It was in the low 40s and we were bundled against the cold, yet the week before, we had been sweltering at a tailgate in Texas.

Although the NDSU tailgates are housed in these multi-level industrial-looking structures, the team spirit abounds with team-colored decor, potted plants, and linen tablecloths all lining the tailgate tables. Like at the southern game-day towns, I swear every single person in the entire town came out to tailgate and cheer their team on. From babies to centenarians and everyone in between, every person was decked-out in their Bison colors—green and yellow. Although the southern tailgaters reign supreme at most things tailgate, particularly warm-weather tailgating, I do believe that, with kind hospitality, NDSU can teach us all a thing or two about commitment to team, because tailgating in the tundra is a whole different game. You must be a sturdy individual of commitment and strong character to dedicate yourself to season after season of tailgating in the dark and freezing cold year after year. Must be that beef stew! Bundle up, and go Bison!

NORWEGIAN BEEF AND VEGGIE STEW (*BRUN LAPSKAUS*)

The invention of the slow cooker is possibly one of the single greatest inventions when it comes to cold-weather tailgating. Effortlessly, this gift of an appliance creates comfort food that makes all other comfort foods jealous. So thick and chunky, you can make the decision on this one—a spoon, a fork, or maybe both. One thing is for sure, the slow cooker and it's low and slow cooking method makes the meat so tender that the very idea of needing a knife is ridiculous.

Makes 8–10 servings

4 Tbsp. butter

4 Tbsp. oil

2½ lbs. beef stewing meat, trimmed and cut into 1-inch cubes

3 cups beef stock

2 large onions, diced

2½ cups celery root or parsnip, peeled and roughly chopped

4 large carrots, peeled and roughly chopped

4 cups potatoes, peeled and cubed

1 large leek, rinsed and cut in thick slices

1 bunch parsley leaves, for garnish

salt and pepper to taste

1. Heat the butter and oil in a large frying pan. Add the beef and brown on each side—you may need to brown the beef in batches. Place the beef in a slow cooker and add the stock. Cook on high for 2 hours.

2. After 2 hours, add the vegetables to the slow cooker. Lower the temperature to medium. Season with salt and pepper to taste. Serve with big chunks of crusty bread and butter. Dipping the bread in the gravy of the stew is highly encouraged.

THE NORTHWEST

THE NORTHWEST IS BEAUTIFUL! Nature abounds, and it shows in the food. The rugged nature of the environment is the base for a down-to-earth tailgate experience with a bit of quiet sophistication. Pick-up trucks, hiking boots, and lumberjack flannel juxtaposed next to some of the most elegant tailgating food around. In some part, the food is typical tailgate food—nachos, wings, etc.—but then there was the first indication that things were going to be a little different in these parts. Someone uncovered a perfectly beautiful charcuterie platter with fancy spreadable local cheeses, fruit, jams, honeycomb, and rustic bread and crackers.

To the side of the tent, several folks excitedly started to gather around the grill. A proud grill master pulled what looked to be a charred bag off the grill. He cracked into the bag, shattering the charred pieces to reveal another smaller set of bags. As he peeled the bags open, they revealed perfectly cooked salmon filets. Everyone grabbed forks and began to chunk away at the filets. As the small crowd enjoyed bite after melty bite, footballs flew, music wafted over the crowd, smiles spread on all the faces, and people ate with excitement and complimented the chef. Experience a little of that same Northwest vibe with the Brown Bag Salmon recipe.

BROWN BAG SALMON

I know, this recipe seems a little out of the ordinary. Honestly, I get it. It is a little different but, don't be afraid, because if you do it right, you will have a delicious tailgate dish that is fresh and smoky and spritzed with lemon… and your fellow tailgaters will be all like, "Wow! Look at you!" It's an easy concept for cooking fish on a grill (fish won't flake and fall through the grates) and it really is super tasty! Seriously, don't live your life in fear, take the bull by the horns or, in this case, grab the fish by the fins and bag it up, grill it up and eat it up!

Makes 4 servings

4 large salmon filets, skin on

olive oil

sea salt and coarsely ground black pepper to taste

4 brown paper lunch bags

1 large brown paper grocery bag

1 spray bottle full of water

lemon wedges

1. Preheat the grill (gas works best for this) to medium indirect heat. If your grill has three burners, be sure the middle burner is turned off. Brush the salmon filets very lightly with olive oil and season with salt and pepper. Place the salmon filets individually in paper lunch bags skin side down. Roll the end of the lunch bags to close them, but not too tightly. Arrange the 4 bags in the center of a larger grocery bag. Roll the open end of the grocery bag to close it, but, not too tightly. Once the grill is hot, place the larger, filled grocery bag in the center of the grill. Cover and grill until salmon filets are cooked through, about 15 minutes, depending on the thickness of the filets. The bag will get black and smolder a bit but won't go up in flames. If it does, use the water bottle to put out flames, but you should not need it.

2. Take the larger paper bag off the grill and place onto a sheet pan. Then pull the smaller bags out of the larger bag, Flip the bags over and place them on a cutting board. Peel the bags off the fillets. The skin should adhere to the bag and peel off. Serve with lemon wedges. Yum!

THE SOUTH

Y'ALL, TAILGATING IN THE SOUTH IS AN EXPERIENCE NOT TO BE MISSED! The atmosphere, the jubilant people, the smells of cauldrons of gumbo (not kidding, cauldrons!), BBQ, grilled sausages, pig roasts, and just so much family, friends, and fun coming together as far as the eye can see. From South Carolina, to Ole Miss, to LSU, to Auburn, to Alabama, to all of the SEC teams, they celebrate in style with decor to beat any tailgates in any other part of the country. They're the trendsetters in the tailgate world. They celebrate their teams like no other!

MIKE'S CRAB, SHRIMP, AND ANDOUILLE GUMBO DIP

My goodness, do they know how to eat and have tailgate fun in the South! If you have a chance to experience a tailgate at LSU or the Grove at Ole Miss, don't miss out, because, by far, in all my tailgate travels, these are some of the best tailgates ever. This recipe represents the flavors of game day in regions of the gulf, southern states with Andouille sausage blended with shrimps, crab, and creole seasoning. These ingredients, with a little okra . . . Well, mother's milk there in Louisiana. P. S. Can you guess who Mike is?

Makes 6–8 servings

1 Tbsp. olive oil

10 oz. Andouille sausage, diced

1 cup finely chopped red and yellow bell pepper; dice and reserve ¼ cup for garnish

¼ cup finely chopped celery

1 cup chopped green onions; dice and reserve ¼ cup for garnish

1 cup frozen sliced okra, chopped

2 garlic cloves, minced

Chicken broth, for deglazing the pan

16 oz. shrimp, peeled, deveined, and chopped

2 tsp. creole seasoning

1 (8-oz.) package cream cheese, softened

6 oz. (about ¾ of a cup) Parmesan cheese, grated, reserve 2 oz. of cheese for mixing with panko and cream cheese

¼ cup white rice, cooked

16 oz. lump crab, drained

2 Tbsp. butter, melted

½ cup panko breadcrumbs

1. Preheat broiler. Heat oil in a 10-inch cast-iron skillet over medium-high heat. Add sausage. Sauté for 2 minutes. Add bell pepper and celery. Sauté for 3 minutes. Add onions, okra, and garlic. Sauté for 3 minutes or until vegetables are tender. Deglaze the pan with chicken broth. Let simmer for 5–7 minutes. Add shrimp and creole seasoning. Sauté for 2 minutes.

2. Reduce heat to low. Add cream cheese, stirring until incorporated. Stir in Parmesan, rice and gently stir in the lump crab. Cook 3 minutes or until mixture is slightly bubbly. Remove from heat.

3. Combine butter with panko and reserved Parmesan cheese. Sprinkle the mixture over the dip and broil for about one minute or until topping is browned. Garnish with green onions and diced red and yellow peppers. Serve with garlic bread, sliced baguette, or crusty toasted bread slices. I like serving it with garlic bread. Over-the-top decadent.

HOT MUFFULETTA DIP

This delicious dip recipe is from the source folks. Direct from the home of my southern friend, Aimee Broussard. She is a two-time cookbook author, food blogger and photographer located in Baton Rouge, LA. If you are looking for an authentic Louisiana recipe, look no further. One thing though, when you serve it up, make sure you serve it with a smile and gracious hospitality because that is how Aimee serves it and with a recipe this authentic, your guests will expect that good ol southern hospitality.

Here's what Aimee says about her recipe:
Made famous by Central Grocery in New Orleans, you'll rarely find an LSU tailgate that doesn't include the Muffuletta in some shape or form; whether a traditional sandwich, maybe some mini sliders . . . or my equally delicious and less messy version, the Hot Muffuletta Dip. All of the unique flavors baked into a casserole dish. Laissez les bon temps rouler!

Makes 10–12 servings

1 (8-oz.) package cream cheese, softened

1 cup Italian olive salad, drained *this can be purchased at most deli's, if you can't find it, use small pitted green olives with pimentos

1 cup diced salami

¼ cup grated Parmesan cheese, plus an additional ¼ cup for topping

¼ cup chopped pepperoncini salad peppers

4 oz. provolone cheese, diced

1 celery rib, finely chopped

½ red bell pepper, chopped

¼ cup fresh parsley, chopped

French bread crostini

1. Preheat the oven to 350 degrees.

2. In a large bowl, combine all of the ingredients except parsley. Spread the mixture into an oven-safe dish. Top with the additional ¼ cup Parmesan cheese. Bake for 25–30 minutes, until cheese is hot and bubbly. Garnish with fresh parsley and serve with French bread crostini.

OPEN FLAME CHAR OYSTERS

It had been my experience that cooked oysters could be a bit funky. I actually, almost didn't try these. I thought they would be Oyster Rockefeller-y which, to me, like their namesake, are too rich. It turns out, these are life-changing. If you have not tried a southern flame charred oyster, you need to make these. You will need an open flame to make these. A grill is great and if you have an open fire pit, even better! You do not need the cast iron oyster pan, you can use a cast iron skillet or another thick bottom pan to make these. Really, if you get a chance, make them. You'll love em'!

Makes 24 Char Oysters

Cheese Topping

2 cups grated Parmesan cheese

1 cup grated mozzarella cheese

2 tablespoons granulated garlic

2 lemons, zested and juiced

Garlic Butter

1 stick unsalted butter

1 cup fresh lemon juice

1/2 cup hot sauce

1/2 cup Worcestershire sauce

1/4 cup chopped garlic

Oysters

24 oysters, shucked on the half shell using a handy-dandy Oyster Knife

Optional dipping bread

1-2 loaves of Italian bread, sliced, buttered and charred on fiery grate!

Cheese Topping

1. Mix the Parmesan, mozzarella, garlic, lemon juice, lemon zest and parsley in a bowl and reserve.

Garlic Butter

2. Place the butter, lemon juice, hot sauce, Worcestershire, chopped garlic, granulated garlic and 1/2 cup water into a small pot on the stove. Slowly melt and whisk ingredients until incorporated. Ladle this into a thermos to be used at the tailgate. Making things ahead makes tailgating a lot more fun for the host, yay!

Preparing your Oysters

3. To make your life easy, prepare the oysters ahead of time. Shuck the oysters. If you have never shucked an oyster before, you will need an oyster shucker, they are inexpensive and available online or any housewares/kitchen store. Place your shucked oysters in a super cool Cast Iron Oyster pan. Top each oyster with a liberal amount of the cheese mixture.

4. Take the top of the shell and place it over the shucked and dressed oyster and wrap the pan with tin-foil. Then place the oysters in a cooler with crushed ice around it. Once you are ready to serve,

bring the oysters out of the cooler for 10 min prior to putting them on the fire.

Charring your oysters

5. First things first, get that fire roaring!

6. Lay down a grate over the flames. Place your prepared oyster pan (foil removed) on the grate for 7-10 min. until the cheese is melted. You will need long tongs and a sturdy oven mitt for pulling the pan off the grate. Remove the oysters from the grate with tongs and place them onto a cookie sheet or a heat-proof surface.

7. Ladle some melted garlic butter over the oysters and serve with grilled bread to soak up the juices and butter! Make sure to spritz with a little lemon to add a touch of brightness. So fresh and delicious!

OR...

8. The above recipe is killer but, if you are not in the mood to shuck and make ahead, I get it. You can simply place unshucked oysters in your pan, then, place on the campfire and wait about 5-10 min. for them to sizzle, spit, and pop open. Serve them with a spritz of lemon, hot sauce and maybe, if you like, cocktail sauce.

THE SOUTHEAST

THE SOUTHEAST IS FULL OF OCEAN BREEZES AND SOUTHERN HOSPITALITY. Some of the best food in the country comes from this region of the US of A. It boasts a spectacular blend of coastal fresh seafood and southern flavors. From shrimp and grits that, literally, will change your life, to the fun and interactive compilation of seasoned red potatoes, corn-on-the-cob, shrimp, crab, and andouille sausage all come together in rustic symphony that is the low-country boil.

My recipe, the Cute Roasted Baby Potatoes Stuffed with Shrimp & Bacon, is a one bite (maybe two, depending on how big the baby potatoes are) that encapsulates my many o' tailgate dining moments in the Southeast.

CUTE ROASTED BABY POTATOES STUFFED WITH SHRIMP AND BACON

A little seafood seasoning and shrimp make these cute potatoes a southeastern coastal treat not to be missed and easy for tailgating. The yum factor is off the charts with a nod to the South Carolina low-country boil mixed with cream cheese and bacon—all sorts of flavor packed in one little baby bite. These are easy to transport. Keep them in the muffin tins for traveling and serving.

Makes 24 servings

Roasted Baby Potatoes with Shrimp and Bacon

24 baby potatoes (red, purple, or golden baby potatoes)

2 Tbsp. olive oil

¼ tsp. kosher salt

¼ tsp. cracked black pepper

Coating (recipe below)

Filling (recipe below)

Coating

2 Tbsp. Dijon mustard

1 Tbsp. Old Bay Seasoning

1 Tbsp. butter, melted

Filling

1 Tbsp. olive oil

1 Tbsp. Dijon mustard

2 Tbsp. Old Bay Seasoning, divided

¼ tsp. kosher salt

¼ tsp. cracked black pepper

3 Tbsp. chives, roughly chopped; half for filling, half for garnish

1 (8 oz.) package onion and chive cream cheese, room temperature

8 oz. grated Monterey Jack cheese

1 lb. cooked shrimp, deveined, tails removed, and chopped small

14 slices bacon, cooked crisp; 10 roughly chopped, 4 broken into big shards for garnish

Roasted Baby Potatoes with Shrimp and Bacon

1. Preheat the oven to 450 degrees.

2. In a large bowl, coat the potatoes with the olive oil, salt, and pepper. Place the potatoes individually in a 24-cup mini-muffin pan.

3. Roast the potatoes for 10 minutes or until soft when pierced. Remove from oven and set aside.

4. While the potatoes are roasting and cooling, prepare the Coating and Filling.

5. When the potatoes have cooled, use a small melon baller or paring knife and small spoon to scoop out a small center portion of the potato (discard the inside portion of the scooped potato). Generously brush the inside and top of each potato with the prepared Coating.

6. Place the tray of brushed potatoes in the oven for 5 minutes to create a glossy, tangy coating on the potato.

7. Stuff each potato with the Filling so that it stands about ¼ inch above the potato, about a tablespoon of filling per baby potato.

8. Put the tray of filled potatoes in the 450-degree oven for 7 minutes. Gently take the potatoes out of the mini-muffin pan with tongs and place on your serving plate.

9. Garnish by inserting a broken shard of crisp bacon into the center of each potato. Add chunky sprinkles of roughly chopped chives. Plating tip: Use a deviled-egg plate or a carry-all with a deviled-egg tray for an on-the-go party.

Coating

10. In a small bowl, stir together mustard, Old Bay Seasoning, and butter.

Filling

11. In a large bowl, combine all of the Filling ingredients, making sure to gently incorporate the shrimp and roughly chopped bacon last.

THE SOUTHWEST

HOT, HOT, HOT!!!!! Hey, Cowpokes, get your ten gallon hat and make your way to the stadium for a home-team hoe down!

The folks in the Southwest like their flavors bold, baby! Unlike the north, the big Southwestern tailgates rarely need portable heaters at their party in the parking lot! Ha! Icy beverages and hearty, spicy bites rule the day. A tailgate staple for a Southwestern party? Any thing Con Queso is a serious must. Check out my version of a Texas-style con queso, you'll be wiping your sweaty brow over every scoop of this hot, cheesy, and chunky dip, but loving every minute of it.

TEXAS GOLD CARNE CON QUESO DIP

Y'all, if you are a foodie, this is the liquid gold that they speak of in Texas. Queso is a standard "must have" staple at all tailgates from Texas, Texas A&M to TCU. Brisket is also one of those staples. This recipe brings the two together in a perfect Texas Gold Carne con Queso. Now, a warning as big as the state: Texas-style brisket takes up to 12 hours to smoke and cook properly. I never smoke a brisket when I make this. I didn't even include the recipe for a brisket because that's just too extra. Please use prepared brisket from the grocery or pick it up at a local BBQ restaurant. Skip that work and buy it prepared. Don't skip the brisket, though—it adds so much authenticity to the dip. It's worth the stop. If you decide to make the brisket . . . well, bless your heart, sweetie!

Makes 10–12 servings

Texas Gold Carne con Queso Dip

1 Tbsp. olive oil

½ white onion, diced

2 jalapenos, seeded and diced

1 garlic clove, minced

½ tsp. ground cumin

½ tsp. black pepper

1 Tbsp. cornstarch

1 cup vegetable broth

1 lb. cheddar cheese, shredded

½ lb. American cheese, shredded

1¼ cups tomatoes, diced; reserve ¼ cup for garnish

salt to taste

Brisket and Beef (recipe below)

guacamole

sour cream

⅛ tsp. chili powder, for garnish

tortilla chips, for dipping

Brisket and Beef

1 Tbsp. olive oil

½ bell pepper, seeded and diced

1 jalapeno, seeded and diced

½ white onion, diced

2 garlic cloves, minced

1 lb. ground beef

1 tsp. ground cumin

1 tsp. chili powder

½ tsp. kosher salt

½ tsp. black pepper

⅛ tsp. cayenne

½ lb. tender chopped brisket
(store-bought or make your own)

Texas Gold Carne con Queso Dip

1. In a small pan, heat the oil on medium heat. Add the onion, jalapeno, and garlic. Cook until the onion is translucent, stirring occasionally, about 5 minutes. Add the onion and jalapeno, and cook until browned. Stir in the cumin, black pepper, and cornstarch. Pour in the broth. Stir constantly until the sauce has thickened. Reduce heat to low. Add the cheese gradually. Add the tomatoes and salt.

2. In a medium bowl, assemble by layering the Brisket and Beef along the bottom of the dish. Pour the queso over the meat. Top with a hearty scoop of the Brisket and Beef, guacamole, sour cream, and reserved diced tomatoes, each in its own spot on top of the queso. Optional: dust the top of the queso with chili powder. Serve warm with chips.

Brisket and Beef

3. In a large skillet, heat the oil on medium-low heat. Add the bell pepper, jalapeno, and onion. Cook until the onion is translucent, stirring occasionally, about 5 minutes. Add the garlic, and cook for 30 more seconds.

4. Add the ground beef, cumin, chili powder, salt, pepper, and cayenne to the skillet. Cook for 15 more minutes or until browned. Stir in cooked and chopped brisket. Remove from heat and drain excess grease.

INDEX

#

50/50 Bar, The 184

1950s' Green Onion Dip, The 55

A

Adobo Lamb Pops with a Char-Roasted Poblano Dipping Sauce 100

Ally's Southern Heat—Spicy Pork Chops 103

B

Bacon & Cheddar Soft Pretzels with Bacon Mustard Dip 92

Bacon Cheeseburger Tater Tot Shepherd's Pie 199

Bacon Pimento Jalapeño Cheese Sandwich on a Pretzel Bun 104

Beth's Chili with Mushrooms & Black Beans 128

Beth's Grilled Apple Cider Donuts with a Maple Glaze 142

Big, Bad Sriracha Fried Chickpea Hummus, The 56

BLT Dip 48

Bloody Mary Jell-O Shot alcohol free, The 34

Brown Bag Salmon 205

Buffalo Cauliflower Nuggets 31

Buffalo Chicken Pizza with Caramelized Red Onions 106

Build an Ultimate Tailgate Char-"Cute"-rie display! 94

C

Caprese Pesto Trifle 108

Cheeseburger Brownie Cupcake, The 152

Cheddar Cheese Dip in a Bread Bowl 91

Cherry Cream Cheese Hand Pies 170

Chili Bar 136

Chipotle Cilantro Deviled Egg 41

Chorizo & Bean Sheet-Pan Nachos 71

Chunky Chili Nachos 72

Chunky Nacho Chili 75

Classic Deviled Egg, The 38

Classic Ham and Swiss Sandwich, The 68

Corned Beef Swiss and Coleslaw Sliders 109

Cute Roasted Baby Potatoes Stuffed with Shrimp and Bacon 213

D

Danish Ebleskiver Waffles 158

Deviled Bacon, The 44

Dijon Sliders with Caramelized Onions 62

DIY Baggie Omelette, The 156

DIY Waffle Brunch Bar 164

Donut and Cupcake Bar 154

Down South Pimento Cheese & Jalapeño Deviled Egg, The 47

E

E3VIP Fire Shrimp 118

Easy Delicious Refried Black Beans 74

Egg and Potato Bundlers—Bacon 110

Egg and Potato Bundlers—Chorizo 112

Egg and Potato Bundlers—Maple
Sausage 113

Elote Guacamole with Cilantro Crema 85

Emily Ellyn's Peanut Butter Caramel
Cheesecake 174

F

Fire-Roasted Jalapeño Deviled Egg 42

Fried Chicken and Waffles Cupcakes 144

G

Game-Day Chili 131

Ginger Sticky Chicken Drummettes 32

Grilled Chicken Wings with Dr. BBQ's
Alabama White Sauce 30

Grilled Corn, Bacon, and Chipotle Dip 49

Grilled Romaine Lettuce with Heirloom
Tomato and Roasted Garlic Vinaigrette ...50

Guacamole 84

H

Honeycrisp Apple Panna Cotta 176

Horseradish Sour Cream 81

Hot Chocolate Grill Cupcake, The 147

Hot Muffuletta Dip 208

Hot Wing Cupcakes with Blue Cheese
Frosting 148

How to Boil an Egg 101 38

How to Build an Ultimate Tailgate
Char-"Cute"-rie 94

How to Cut a Deviled Egg with Fab
Style 38

How to Pack a Cooler 23

I

Italian Chili Mac 132

J

Jay's Blackberry Bone-in Boston Butt 114

Jerry James Stone's Coconut, Lime, and
Avocado Popsicles 173

K

Kari's Vegan Loaded Nachos 77

Kerry's Big Bite Pastrami with Pancetta
Giardiniera and Artichoke Spread 122

Killer Chunk Chocolate Cake with Chocolate
Buttercream Frosting 178

L

Lamar Moore's KFC—Korean Fried
Chicken 116

"Lobster Roll" Deviled Egg 40

M

Mac Daddy Mac & Cheese 65

Meatloaf Cupcake, The 150

Mexican Braised Short Ribs 78

Mexican Braised Short Rib Sheet-Pan
Nachos 79

Mike's Crab, Shrimp, and Andouille Gumbo
Dip 207

Mini Apple Pies in a Jar 181

Momma's Potato Salad 119

N

Norwegian Beef and Veggie Stew
(Brun Lapskaus) 203

O

Open Flame Char Oysters 210

P

Peach Bread with Cheddar Crumble 182

Pickled Red Onions 83

Pimento Cheese Jalapeños Wrapped in
    Bacon 64

Pomegranate Guacamole 87

Poppin' Popcorn Recipes 138

R

Roasted Poblano and Cheddar Cornbread in
    a Cast-Iron Skillet 141

Roasted Tomatillo Guacamole 88

Rosemary & Roasted Garlic White Bean
    Dip 53

S

Serrano Sweet Pepper Jelly 82

Shrimp and Peach Ceviche 36

Slow Cooker Chicago Italian Beef
    Sandwiches 200

Slurping Watermelon, The 187

S'mores Cookie Sandwich 175

Southern Sweet Tea 193

Spiced Crab 54

Sushi Donuts 37

Sweet Heat Pulled Pork and Udon
    Noodles 120

T

Texas Gold Carne con Queso Dip 215

Touchdown Brunch...................................160

Touchdown Brunch DIY Waffle Brunch
    Bar 164

V

Vegan Queso 80

VV's Philly Cheesesteak Sliders 197

W

Waffle Bites 160

Warning! Ridiculously Addictive Blue Cheese
    Kettle Chips 67

White Chicken Chili Mac Bread Bowls 135

Whitney's Gator Corndogs 194

Y

Yo, It's Pepperoni Pizza Dip 57

NOTES

ABOUT THE PHOTOGRAPHER
MARK HARTMAN

Mark Hartman is a photographer based outside of Chicago and brings both his eye for detail and keen sense of humor to every shoot he does. It was after stints in advertising agencies, building brands for a number of companies, that Mark's love for commercial photography began. Over the years, he worked with a number of accomplished photographers behind the scenes and eventually picked up the camera himself, putting much of what he learned in advertising to work for his clients.

Currently, Mark's primary photography focus is with food-related brands and restaurants, with recent work for Bahama Breezes, Native Foods Cafe, Anheuser Busch and Purina Foods.

Mark's work has been featured in *Chicago Tribune, LA Weekly*, MarthaStewartLiving.com, Vegan News, and Fender Bender magazine to name a few. When not behind the lens, you can find Mark trying out different restaurants, exploring new whiskey or cooking at home with his wife Jen and their plethora of pets.

HartmanPictures.com

ABOUT THE AUTHOR
BETH PETERSON

How does one become a tailgate food expert, anyway? As the former owner of a sports-themed restaurant, an award-winning recipe developer, TV competitor (alum of Fox's *Masterchef*, FYI's *Food Champs*, and Food Network's *Cutthroat Kitchen*), all while being the team mom at home, Beth Peterson landed the envied job of Tailgate Recipe Developer and Brand Cheerleader for Sam's Club and Coke Zero and as a tailgate spokesperson at *ESPN College GameDay*. The experience had Beth to participating in some of the biggest college tailgates around the country. She learned about the variety and tradition in tailgate foods from regions throughout the US. She found an inspired "leveled-up" tailgate experience, with everything from the hottest hot wings to lobster nachos, to Scandinavian soups from way up north in Fargo, to giant fancy southern cakes in the southern college town of Baton Rouge and then, there was the epic over-the-top low-country boil in South Carolina #gogamecocks!! All of this deliciousness was done-up with incredible style, think chandeliers, red carpets and ice sculptures! It's a go-big or go-home mentality that rules the tailgate experience and it's all brought to you in the pages of this book! Beth lives in the Midwest (Go Bears!) and is mom to one non-football-interested daughter and two very football-interested sons (Go Bulldogs! #63, Go Hawks! #90), as well as, her good boy, Clyde the German Shepherd and a sweet/grumpy Wheatie dog named Stella.

www.thetailgatecookbook.com